At some point in life, we all have to face up to the subject of death, dying and funerals, either for ourselves or somebody else. This book provides a one-stop source of valuable and up to date advice, written by a qualified and experienced civil funeral celebrant, Sarah Chapman M.I.C.F.

Sarah has helped many people to talk about death and dying and to create and lead them through all kinds of funeral ceremonies. All that knowledge and experience comes together now in a book that will ease you through, with her own personal touches, some of the most difficult decisions that you are ever likely to face.

Clearly written and set out, this is the one book that you probably don't want to read but really must.

Sue Holden

Sarah Chapman

Funeral Arranging and End-of-Life Decisions

A STEP-BY-STEP GUIDE

The Book Guild Ltd

First published in Great Britain in 2022 by
The Book Guild Ltd
Unit E2 Airfield Business Park,
Harrison Road, Market Harborough,
Leicestershire. LE16 7UL
Tel: 0116 2792299
www.bookguild.co.uk
Email: info@bookguild.co.uk
Twitter: @bookguild

Typeset in 11pt Sabon MT

Printed on FSC accredited paper
Printed and bound in Great Britain by 4edge Limited

ISBN 978 1914471 988

British Library Cataloguing in Publication Data.
A catalogue record for this book is available from the British Library.

For my loved ones

Contents

Part 2: Funeral Organising

Part 3: The Funeral Ceremony

Part 4: Specialised Ceremonies

Part 5: Planning and Wishes

Part 6: My Plan

Part 7: Conclusion

Part 8: Helpful Resources

Introduction

Death is the destination we all share.

—Anon

As we travel through life, we experience major milestones (rites of passage) that mark changes as we pass from one phase to another, such as birth, becoming an adolescent, graduation, leaving home, getting married, retirement and death.

A rite of passage is more than just a new beginning, or a new phase or chapter. It is the ending and leaving behind of an old phase that cannot be revisited, which is why it is momentous and important to mark it. It also provides a sense of belonging, as a rite of passage is usually performed with family, friends or community.

Ceremonies connect us with the past of our forebears and can be passed from one generation to the next, which helps to confirm the continuity of life. There are traditions that state the rules and rituals regarding dress, place and time, but there is always space to create new rituals to pass on to future generations.

Who This Book Is For

The purpose of this book is to give you a step-by-step guide to what happens when someone dies and the choices available to enable you to create a funeral that is personal to them.

This book takes away the fear and confusion that happens when you are faced with organising the funeral of a loved one and gives you control in creating a heartfelt ceremony to celebrate their life. It will also give you ideas for how to plan your own funeral in a way that is unique to you. There is a section on choices around end-of-life planning to help you make your own decisions.

How to Use This Book

If you read from beginning to end, you will have enough information to arrange your loved one's funeral and pre-plan your own end-of-life ceremony. Each section stands alone so that you can find information easily and refer back to it. I have also included handy top tips throughout.

You will find a Helpful Resources section (see Part 8), containing links to useful online resources and addresses, recognising that everyone's needs are different.

This book includes real stories, so to preserve anonymity of the people described, all names have been changed. Where possible, I have used the words 'deceased' or 'loved one' when talking about the person who has died, and I refer to 'families and friends' as anyone who is regarded as close to the deceased.

Sharing your decisions can be difficult, but if you highlight your choices in this book and hand it to your family and friends, they will know exactly what you want. You can also use the My Plan section (see Part 6) to note down your wishes for your own end-of-life ceremony and decisions for after your death.

Over the years, I have talked to many families who wished they had been aware of the choices available to them when their loved ones had died, and been able to discuss them beforehand. I hope that, by reading this book, you will be less afraid to talk about funerals and to plan for what is inevitable. I also hope that you find the subject thought-provoking and inspiring, enabling you to find the confidence to suggest new ideas for celebrating end-of-life ceremonies.

Background

At birth we board the train and meet our parents,
and we believe they will always travel by our side.
As time goes by, other people will board the train;
and they will be significant...

...We do not know at which station we ourselves will step down. So,
we must live in the best way, love, forgive, and offer the best of who we
are. It is important to do this because when the time comes for us to
step down and leave our seat empty we should leave behind beautiful
memories for those who will continue to travel on the train of life.

I wish you all a joyful journey.

—Anon, 'The Train of Life'

I had always found funerals to be depressing and, usually, not about the person who we were mourning. I attended traditional funerals led by someone who had not met the deceased's family, and even one funeral where the vicar talked about Edgar all the way through when the deceased was, in fact, called William! At one stage in my twenties

I attended three funerals in a row that all had the same words and music, with only a fleeting reference to the life that had ended.

At my mother-in-law's funeral in 2012, I was pleased to have been asked to read a poem – one that I had found in her bedside table in an old purse. As the ceremony was taken by a celebrant and not the local vicar, I didn't know what to expect. I used my skills as a drama and music teacher to explore the meaning in the words of the poem as I wanted to let family and friends know what it must have meant to her. The ceremony was beautiful, heartfelt and highly personal, and I realised that there was a different way to celebrate a life, which included her story, her wishes and her beliefs. The crematorium was full of her family and friends, and there was laughter as well as tears. By the end of the ceremony, we all felt we had sent her on her way with love, affection and dignity.

I realised that I wanted to give that same feeling to other people and, when the celebrant drew me aside and asked whether I had thought of becoming a celebrant, I was overjoyed. He sent me the details of Civil Ceremonies Ltd. in Cambridgeshire and this is where I completed two national qualifications – the NOCN Level 3 Diploma in Funeral Celebrancy (RQF) in 2012 and the NOCN Level 3 Diploma in Naming and Couples Celebrancy (RQF) in 2013. It was a challenge to begin a new career at fifty-five, but I have never regretted that decision.

Since then, my life has been enriched by meeting over seven hundred families, sharing their stories and helping each of them to have a personal ceremony that is perfect for them. I have also found a community of celebrants and colleagues who have supported me and acted as guides, making me realise that teamwork makes us stronger than the sum of our individual parts.

I have raised awareness by contributing to discussions about death and funerals on the radio and attended Death Cafes to open up the (sometimes taboo) discussion about what happens at the end of life. I have also enabled people to create and plan their own funeral wishes. In 2021, I started on my journey to become an end-of-life doula and I am a member of End of Life Doula UK.

My life has been immeasurably enriched by working with bereaved families. In supporting them, they have acted as guides throughout my career, and I have learnt that you cannot judge a book by its cover. I have also learnt over the years to be an understanding listener rather than a mender of problems. None of us is ordinary; each unique individual is extraordinary in their own way.

It is important to me to know that I am creating and delivering ceremonies that families want and, out of all the treasured feedback I have received over the years, these two testimonials stand out:

> *I would recommend Sarah to anyone wishing to conduct a sensitive personal service for their loved one. She listened carefully to all our suggestions and requests and really tried to get to know the family and the deceased so as to make the service as personal and pertinent as possible. Sarah was also extremely helpful with any advice she had to offer us – always given in an understanding and considerate way and obviously based on considerable experience.*

Thanks to Sarah's management, both the private family funeral and the huge thanksgiving service we held four weeks later were professional and empathetic events. Everything both my family and myself could have wanted. Sarah acted like a supporting friend and was very comfortable to be with. A very sad day for us now has become a happier memory.

PART 1

When Someone
You Love Dies

1.1

What to Do
After the Death

Death is not extinguishing the light.
It is putting out the lamp because the dawn has come.

—Rabindranath Tagore

What Do You Do When Someone Dies?

It is always a shock when a loved one dies. Your entire world may change, however long you have been prepared for their death. You may feel a variety of different emotions like anger, guilt or sadness. It is important to remember that everyone grieves differently and there is no right or wrong way to grieve.

Top Tip

Turn to your friends and family to support you by asking them for practical help with shopping, cooking and making arrangements.

At Home

When someone dies at home and it is expected, note the time of death. Take the time to say goodbye to them and, when you are ready, call your loved one's doctor. There will need to be two doctors to verify the death. During Covid, this might be done virtually via FaceTime, if you or your family feel confident to do so; if not, a professional must carry this out in person.

The doctor should be able to issue a Medical Certificate of Cause of Death (MCCD), which details the cause of death and is required to register the death.

In a Hospital or Care Home

If the person died in hospital, after a while they will be taken to the mortuary and they will remain there for a while. If they have died in a care home or hospice, the duty funeral director will care for them at their premises until you decide on the next step. In each case, the doctor will issue the MCCD.

Take Your Time

If you are sitting with your loved one, then do not feel you have to leave them straight away. You may want to say your goodbyes and share memories in whatever way is right for you. Depending on circumstances, always remember that there is no rush.

It is entirely your own choice and is not compulsory, but some families show their love and respect by combing their loved one's hair, or washing or massaging oil into their hands and feet. You can create a sense of ritual by playing music and lighting candles, gathering with others or inviting visitors to sit with you. This offers the opportunity for storytelling, sharing thoughts, laughter and tears.

Leyla

When Leyla died, her family were sitting around her bed, holding hands. They lit candles around the room and sent their loving thoughts to Leyla. Her niece continued to massage Leyla's hands then kissed them, before quietly placing them under the quilt.

After half an hour of sitting quietly, her brother started to sing 'Amazing Grace' and gradually everyone in the room joined in. He told me that they had sung it at their mother's funeral and it had now become a constant in their lives. They stayed, drinking tea and sharing memories, for another hour. Gradually, one by one, they kissed Leyla on the cheek, said, "Goodbye, Leyla, sweet dreams," and went home, promising to provide meals for Leyla's husband over the next few days.

Pushing Up The Daisies (www.pushingupthedaisies.org.uk) is a charity based in Scotland that provides information and support to those who want to keep the body of their loved one at home (or bring them back home) after their death. You can download a booklet from their website or phone them for advice. They suggest being prepared by getting together a home kit before your loved one dies and asking friends and family to help. All the details can be found on their website.

Unexpected Death

If the death is unexpected, call the ambulance services immediately by dialling 999. The operator will provide instructions on what you need to do next.

Make sure you have to hand your loved one's advanced decision document or locate the MedicAlert jewellery on their body. Paramedics should know to look for the Lions Club International 'Message in a Bottle' in the fridge when entering someone's house so that they can locate their end-of-life decisions, or the advance decision may be registered on their system. If there is no advance decision in place, the paramedics will attempt resuscitation before confirming the death. The paramedics will contact the police if they feel it is necessary to do so.

Acting on behalf of the coroner if the death is unexpected, the police will arrange for a duty funeral director or one of your own choice to collect your loved one, usually by private ambulance, and take the body into their care. The coroner (or procurator fiscal in Scotland) may order a post-mortem examination or inquest to determine the cause of death and then issue the MCCD.

Organ Donation

Organ donation is now automatic as the law requires all adults to become organ donors when they die. Your loved one may have stated which organs they are happy to donate. However, most people do not die in circumstances that make it possible for them to donate their organs. In fact, only around 1 in 100 people who die in the UK are usually able to be donors, and are typically those who have died in a hospital intensive care unit or emergency department. However, if it was your loved one's wish, the sooner that donation takes place, the better the transplant outcome will be.

Donating the Body to Science

If your loved one has asked for their body to be donated to science, all the paperwork will need to have been completed before their death, so make sure you check their funeral wishes and will beforehand, just in case. Under some circumstances a medical school may not be able to accept their body if they have certain health conditions or have recently undergone surgery. If this is the case, a funeral will need to be arranged instead.

Miscarriage

Every pregnancy loss is different and you may feel unable to talk to anyone about what has happened but, whatever your feelings, you are not alone. If you feel you cannot talk to family or friends, reaching out to a good counsellor can help you understand and find strategies to help you cope.

You can access a counsellor through your GP, hospital or a charity. There is also a network of support group volunteers who have personal experience of pregnancy loss, so have a real understanding of what you are going through.

If your baby died before the twenty-fourth week of pregnancy, you do not need to register the death. Some hospitals will give you a certificate in memory of your baby if you ask. If they don't offer it, you can ask a nurse or midwife on the ward, the hospital chaplain or in the bereavement office.

After a miscarriage you may feel that you would like to mark your baby's brief life and find a way of remembering them. There are online memorial spaces such as Stars of Remembrance on the Miscarriage Association website (miscarriageassociation.org.uk). You can write a message in memory of your baby with their name and date and they will add a star to the online sky and send you a unique ID so that you can visit at any time.

Babies and Stillbirth

If your baby dies after the twenty-fourth week of pregnancy, your midwife will give you information about registering the death and suggest support groups. There is also a charity called Daddy's with Angels (www.daddyswithangels.org) who provide support and guidance to all family members affected by the loss of a child at any age, especially for bereaved dads.

Milly

When Jasmin and Pete's baby died soon after her birth, they were shown into a special room in the hospital that was made available to support bereaved families who have experienced the loss of a baby. They named their baby Milly, after her grandmother, washed her and dressed her in the clothes and blanket they had brought with them. They spent time holding Milly and taking photographs, creating special memories for the months and years afterwards.

There are charities such as Stillbirth and Neonatal Death Charity, SANDS (www.sands.org.uk) that offer local group meetings, literature and additional support to relieve the mental suffering from those who have lost a baby. They even offer a free Always Loved Never Forgotten Memory Box for parents to create and save precious memories before saying goodbye. Before the funeral, you can take your baby home in a 'cuddle cot' to keep them cool. Remember that you and your partner may have different ideas, so do what is right for you.

Top Tip

Take time to ask questions and consider all the choices you have before making a decision about what is best for you and your loved one.

There are charities that also provide cribs, graveside

dressing (www.cherishedgowns.org.uk) and various other items if you have chosen a burial, and most cemeteries have a special area for babies' graves. If there are restrictions about headstones you can make your own arrangements for a plaque somewhere else in the cemetery.

Some crematoria have special facilities to protect ashes, even for babies who are very small, so asking in advance will help you choose the correct crematorium for you.

1.2

Registering
the Death

I read of a man who stood to speak at the funeral of a friend.
He referred to the dates on the tombstone from the beginning... to the end.

He noted that first came the date of birth
and spoke of the following date with tears,
but he said what mattered most of all
was the dash between those years.
For that dash represents all the time they spent alive on earth
and now only those who loved them know what that little line is worth.

—Linda Ellis

Registering the death should be done within five days by the Registrar of Births, Deaths and Marriages, which is situated at the local register office. It will take about thirty minutes.

If someone dies at home, the death should be registered at the register office in the district in which they lived. This can be done in person or, since Covid, by scanning and emailing the documents. The death certificate will then be posted back to you.

If the death took place in a hospital, nursing home or other public building, the death must be registered at the register office for the district in which the hospital or home is situated. Make sure you have the correct address of the place your loved one died so that you can find the appropriate register office.

If the cause of death is unclear, a coroner will hold a post-mortem and, maybe, an inquest. The coroner then informs the registrar and will issue an interim death certificate for probate purposes.

Wherever you register the death, you must take with you the medical certificate of death, as the death cannot be registered until the registrar has seen this. If possible, you should also take your loved one's NHS medical card and birth and marriage certificates.

The registrar will then ask you to provide the following information:

- The date and place of death
- The full name of the person (including maiden name) and their last address
- Their date and place of birth
- Their occupation
- The full name, date of birth and job of a living or dead spouse or civil partner
- If the person was still married, the date of birth of their husband or wife
- Whether the person was receiving a pension or other social security benefits.

Once you have registered the death, the registrar will give you the Certificate of Registration of Death, 'white form' or 'BD8 form'; the Certificate for Burial or Cremation, or 'green form' to allow for burial or cremation to take place; and, for a small fee, the death certificate.

Top Tip

Make sure you obtain a minimum of seven copies of the death certificate as you will need them to cancel bank accounts, etc.

Philip

Barbara's husband Philip had been suffering from cancer and he made sure that all his documents were ready in a folder. After his death, Barbara went to their local register office to register Philip's death. She knew she had everything she needed and was amazed at how easy and efficient it was.

Top Tip

Locate all the documents required to register the death and put them into a folder together.

Death Abroad

If a death takes place abroad it must be registered according to the law of that country. The death should also be reported to the British Consul, who may be able to arrange for the death to be also registered in the UK.

The cost of returning the body to the UK may be covered by any travel insurance taken out by the person. If the death took place on a package holiday, the tour operator should be able to help with arrangements. If the person died on a foreign ship or aircraft, you must register the death in the country where the ship or aircraft is registered.

1.3

——

Informing People and Organisations

After all, to the well-organised mind,
death is but the next great adventure.

—J.K. Rowling, *Harry Potter and the Philosopher's Stone*

Family and Friends

There will be many people you need to contact about the death and the funeral or memorial service. If you have a long list, ask a friend or family member to do this for you so that you can concentrate on the ones you would like to talk to personally. If the deceased was a member of any groups, ask one member of the group to be responsible for calling all the others.

Place a notice in the local paper and on social media, if appropriate. You will reach more people this way but, if you do not want them all to come to the funeral, do not include the details.

Top Tip

Make sure you know where your loved one's address book is kept – and their computer password.

When Andrew's father died, he had to employ a computer expert to bypass the password on his dad's computer. This was the only way he could find all his father's contacts!

Social Media

Your loved one may have made a social media will, containing non-sensitive information about the accounts they use and what they would like to happen to them and the content they contain. They may want some social media accounts to be deactivated, or for you to recover photographs stored online for the funeral.

If there is no will or funeral wishes, an immediate family member or other authorised person can decide to have the social media profile deleted. The help section on each social media site will offer advice, and you may need to show a birth or death certificate of the deceased and proof that you are a lawful representative of the person.

Tell Us Once Service

When you register the death, the registrar will explain about the Tell Us Once service (www.gov.uk/after-a-death/organisations-you-need-to-contact-and-tell-us-once). Tell Us Once is a free government service that helps with practical issues. You are given a unique reference number so you can use the service yourself online or by phone. When activated, they notify all relevant authorities and official bodies of the death, saving the family from having to make countless phone calls notifying them of their bereavement.

Top Tip

You will need to inform banks, utility companies and landlords or housing associations of the death yourself.

DWP Bereavement Service

In England and Wales, the Department for Works and Pensions (DWP) Bereavement Service allows you to report a death to the DWP in a single phone call, which will cover all the DWP benefits the person who died was getting.

The Bereavement Service can also do a benefit check to find out if the next of kin can claim any benefits and take a claim for bereavement benefits or a funeral payment over the phone.

Care for Pets

The Cinnamon Trust (www.cinnamon.org.uk) has a national network of community service volunteers who provide practical help when any aspect of day-to-day care for pets poses a problem – for example, walking the dog for someone at the end of their life. They also provide long-term care for pets whose owners have died, as long as arrangements are made between owners and the Trust well in advance. Owners then have peace of mind in the knowledge that their beloved companion will have a safe and happy future.

The Dogs Trust (www.dogstrust.org.uk) will arrange for your loved one's dog to be taken to the nearest rehoming centre, where it will be looked after until they can find a suitable new owner.

The Cats Protection (www.cats.org.uk) offers a free service called Cat Guardians. They will look after your loved one's cat until they find a suitable new owner.

PART 2

Funeral Organising

2.1

———

Organising
the Funeral

Don't cry because it's over, smile because it happened.

—Dr. Seuss

Your loved one may have left instructions about the type of funeral they wanted in their will or funeral wishes document. If they didn't make their wishes known, you will need to decide whether to have a funeral director or ask your family and friends to help. Initially, asking a funeral director to care for the body at their premises as a stand-alone service gives you time to consider how you want to proceed with the rest of the arrangements.

Funeral Directors

If you do decide to have a funeral director then recommendations from other people can help. The funeral director's job is to arrange the details and handle the logistics of funerals. Together with the family, funeral directors establish the location, dates and times of wakes, memorial services and burials. They do not decide on the content of the funeral ceremony.

All funeral directors, by law from June 2021, have to display their 'standard price list' for 'attended' and 'unattended' funerals on their website, which must be only one click away from the home page. They also have to provide printed copies of their prices to customers, if requested. This information must be provided in advance of a family member committing to purchase a service so that people know the price they will be charged and the key terms of business – for example, if a deposit is required.

There will be an extra charge for 'prices on request', which are costs for a funeral service that are paid to third parties, such as florists, celebrants and burial fees. The funeral director will usually charge you for them and then pay the suppliers themselves.

With this in mind, talk to the funeral director about the type of funeral you would like and how much you would like to be involved. Ask for quotes from two or three companies, with a full breakdown of their costs, before you decide. It is important that you choose only the parts of their services that you want. If, for example, you do not want a fleet of limousines then let them know.

If you wish to view your loved one, some funeral directors advise on embalming, but this is a highly invasive procedure and is not essential, as long as the body is cared for sensitively and kept cold. Check with the funeral director whether you can visit your loved one out of working hours, if that is important to you.

Even if your loved one is already with a funeral director, you are within your rights to change your mind. The Natural Death Centre website (www.naturaldeath. org.uk) has up-to-date and unbiased information, help, support, advice and guidance in arranging a funeral, either for yourself or for someone close to you.

Always check that the funeral directors are fully qualified and have had regular inspections. The most important requirement is that the funeral director and their staff come across as both caring and professional, they listen to you carefully and don't try to sell you extra products that you do not need.

Remember that knowledge is power so that you can make informed choices about what is right for you and your loved one. You are the client and the bill payer and it is wise to shop around for the most competitive prices and the best fit for your family.

Top Tip

At the first meeting, funeral directors may ask for your choice of music, which, for some families, is too soon. Remember that you are free to change your mind at any time, so do not feel bound by your early decisions.

Self-Organised Funerals

You can arrange a funeral without a funeral director. If you want to organise the funeral yourself, the Natural Death Centre or cemeteries and crematorium department of your local authority can offer help and guidance.

Keeping a body at home before a funeral is rare in the UK, but it is not illegal. In fact, sixty years ago it was commonplace to have your loved one at home. The most important consideration is temperature. Some funeral directors will be happy to help with the aspects that might be difficult for an individual family, such as completing the necessary paperwork or supplying air-conditioning units in the summer months to keep a body cool. They can also provide a Flexmort – an ice pack to keep your loved one cold.

There are companies that offer support and guidance in how to care for your loved one at home after they die. Home Funeral Network (www.homefuneralnetwork. org.uk) and Only With Love (www.onlywithlove.co.uk) also help you create a ceremony and arrange a family-led funeral.

Wendii

In 2012, Wendii Miller took this one step further and took on officialdom, collected her mother's body in a camper van and spent the next three days working through her grief. She said:

> *I drove Ma around to her friends so they could say goodbye, and I took her down to her*

> *favourite beach. I very much doubt, being dead,*
> *that she was bothered one way or another, but*
> *it did ME a helluva lot of good. After all, I was*
> *the one suffering now. Hers was over.*

Wendii even dug her mother's grave herself, fortified by tea and chocolate cake supplied by the owner of the burial ground.

Direct Cremations

Since Covid in 2020, more people have requested direct cremations. The deceased is cremated shortly after death, without embalming, viewing or family visits. This is the cheapest and most affordable cremation option.

With direct cremation, the funeral director takes care of the essential elements of a funeral, including cremation fees, doctor's fees, care of your loved one and transportation to the crematorium. It also means you can choose your own way to remember someone with a memorial ceremony later, at a place and time that suits you.

Children at Funerals

Following a death, there is such a bewildering array of emotions and sometimes trying not to upset your children, however young, by keeping it from them may feel right. For advice and support local to you contact the Child Bereavement Network (www.childhoodbereavementnetwork.org.uk).

However, it is helpful to talk with honesty and explain what has happened in a way that a child can understand. Including children in the funeral planning and giving them choices may help them feel valued and a part of this big event. They can help to choose the coffin and place a note or object inside, or choose special poems and music that they think their loved one would like.

Of course, it is up to you, but as long as you prepare them well and guide them through the day they will have a positive memory of the funeral. Explain that the funeral is about celebrating and remembering the person who has died and surrounding them with love. Tell them that they will be there, along with other family and friends, and it is okay to express their feelings, to cry and even laugh. If they are excluded, they may think that death is frightening and grief must not be talked about.

Top Tip

It is fine if your child doesn't want to attend the funeral, but they can still be asked to help choose the poems and music.

To help older children understand death, the book *Water Bugs and Dragonflies* by Doris Stickney is highly recommended. It describes the journey taken by a water bug crawling up a lily stalk and disappearing from sight. The remaining water bugs are mystified and only when they have climbed the lily stalk themselves do they understand the transformation into another world. The book ends with the words, 'And the dragonfly winged off happily into its wonderful new world of sun and air.'

Help with the Cost of a Funeral

Pre-Paid Funeral Plan or Funeral Insurance
Some people may already have paid a funeral director or a funeral care company with a funeral plan. You will have to use that funeral director, or one from an approved list, to arrange the funeral, but it is a good idea to check exactly what's covered by the plan as you will need to cover the rest of the costs yourself.

Funeral insurance, sometimes known as an over-fifties plan, pays out a fixed lump sum to cover the cost of the funeral. Again, check how much you will receive as it may not cover the full cost of the funeral.

Top Tip

Check your loved one's papers for a copy of a funeral plan or insurance. They may have stored it with their will, with a family solicitor or at their bank.

Bank Account

Your loved one may have left money in their own bank account to pay for the funeral but, unfortunately, any account will be frozen when the bank or building society is told of their death. If you cannot ask the executor or administrator of their estate to access the money, you will need to show a copy of the death certificate and an invoice for the funeral costs with your name on it. The bank or building society will then pay the essential funeral bills directly to the company providing the service.

Funeral Expenses Payment

If you live in England, Wales or Northern Ireland and are receiving benefits, you may be eligible for a Funeral Expenses Payment from the government (www.gov.uk/funeral-payments) to help you pay your costs. It is non-refundable and will need to be claimed within six months of the funeral taking place. If you live in Scotland, you may be able to apply for a Funeral Support Payment instead (www.mygov.scot/funeral-support-payment).

Children's Funeral Fund

If you are arranging and paying for the funeral of a child under eighteen or a stillborn baby, you may be able to get help from the Children's Funeral Fund for England (www.gov.uk/child-funeral-costs). The payment is not means-tested and it covers burial or cremation fees, including the cost of a doctor's certificate. It will also pay part of the cost towards a coffin, shroud or casket. The Fund does not pay for the funeral director or celebrant's fees, transport, flowers or the order of service. The fees can be claimed directly by the burial or cremation provider – you should not be charged.

Some funeral directors and celebrants offer their services at reduced costs for children's funerals, so make sure you check beforehand.

Child Funeral Charity

The Child Funeral Charity (www.childfuneralcharity.org. uk) was set up to help families in England and Wales who are arranging a funeral for a baby or child aged sixteen or under. The charity will cover any part of the funeral not covered by the Children's Funeral Fund for England, such as the flowers, orders of ceremony and plaques.

Only professionals who have knowledge of the bereaved family and their circumstances, such as the funeral director, celebrant or faith representative, bereavement nurse or midwife or another medical professional, can refer families to this Fund.

Environmental Health Department

If there are no relatives to be found, the environmental health department in your local council registers the death and sorts out the funeral, which will include:

- The collection of the deceased
- A basic coffin
- Fees for the crematorium or burial
- One suitable vehicle to transport the deceased
- A basic service at the crematorium by a local funeral director.

2.2

Burial or Cremation

Lay me in some leafy loam where, sheltered from the cold
Little seeds investigate and tender leaves unfold.
There kindly and affectionately, plant a native tree
To grow resplendent before God and hold some part of me.

—Pam Ayres, 'Woodland Burial'

Burial or Cremation

Choosing between a burial or cremation is the next step. Many people find that it is comforting to have a place to pay their respects, and graves in cemeteries or natural burial grounds offer family and friends a place to visit their loved ones. However, after a cremation, the ashes are returned to the family and they have more time to decide what to do with them; maybe scattering them in a favourite place or interring them in a family burial plot. Regardless of whether a person has been buried or cremated, families can grieve wherever they feel they are closest to their loved one.

The actual burial or cremation does not need to take place on the day of the funeral ceremony, but if you decide to do this then any venue that agrees to having the coffin and is big enough for all your family and friends can be chosen for the ceremony, such as a church, crematorium, cemetery, woodland burial ground, community venue, local hotel or even your own home.

Always check beforehand that the venue is private so that members of the public don't wander in. A hotel or restaurant can also offer refreshments afterwards for your guests and provides a relaxed environment with no set time limit. You may even choose to have the ceremony in your own home or garden, surrounded by your loved one's belongings and favourite pets.

Top Tip

A marquee or yurt can extend your home if you need more space and will provide shelter if it rains.

After the ceremony, the coffin will be taken to your chosen crematorium or burial place, possibly with just close family or friends, before you join your guests back at the wake.

A memorial service is a ceremony with no coffin present that can take place any time before or after the funeral. It can be held where everyone can get together or outside at your loved one's favourite spot. The decision will come down to what's right for you and your family and will be based on your situation, including budget, personal beliefs and religion.

What Happens at a Crematorium?

Crematoria encompass all beliefs, customs and traditions. The chapel can usually hold up to a hundred mourners, with additional space in the chapel for people to stand. A traditional organ and organist are usually available, there is often a public address system and your choice of music will be played by the staff on your behalf.

Top Tip

Most crematoria have facilities to show a slide show of photographs while a favourite piece of music is playing. This can be played at any time during the ceremony.

For larger congregations, the ceremony can be broadcast to an outdoor covered area so that people can still see and hear the service even if they are not in the chapel. Most crematoria have disabled access and an induction loop system to help people who use a hearing aid or loop listener to listen more clearly.

Nearly all crematoria have webcams set up in the chapel, and a livestream of the funeral can be watched by families or friends living abroad or unable to attend, allowing them to observe and take comfort from anywhere in the world. This has become more popular during the Covid pandemic, where numbers of mourners attending a funeral have been limited. The broadcasts are live but can also be watched for seven days after the funeral. DVD and CD audio recordings may also be available after the funeral.

Services at crematoria have time restrictions. The service slot can be forty-five minutes long, but this includes time to enter and leave the chapel, so you actually have only thirty minutes for the ceremony. If you feel that you need more time, you can book a double slot.

Fees vary depending on whether you have a full attended ceremony or just a committal for a direct cremation. Services at the beginning and end of the day tend to be cheaper, while ceremonies on Saturdays can be more expensive.

Some crematoria are happy to show you around with prior arrangement so you can see what happens on the day and even what happens behind the scenes. It is worth contacting your local crematoria as it may reassure you that coffins are not reused afterwards and there are strict rules in place about keeping everyone's ashes separate.

Open-Air Pyres

In 2010, Mr Ghai, a British Hindu, won his battle at the Court of Appeal, which ruled that he had a right to be cremated in accordance with his beliefs. Mr Ghai's legal challenge was on religious grounds, but it is possible for anyone to choose a natural cremation, whatever their personal beliefs. The Natural Death Centre has up-to-date information to help you decide.

The Environmental Impact of Gas Crematoria

Choosing an environmentally friendly option may be important to you, so researching the facts about cremation will be useful. In the UK, a large percentage of people are now cremated in over six hundred cremator machines. Nearly all of these machines are gas-powered, producing tonnes of carbon each year. The UK government is now aiming for a large reduction in greenhouse gas emissions by the end of the decade. To achieve this aim, they are installing electric cremators into brand-new facilities that run on a green energy tariff, releasing much less carbon into the local environment than a conventional gas cremator.

Mercury, from tooth fillings, is also a problem. Exposure to the mercury pollution from crematoria is linked to damage to the brain and nervous system and fertility issues. Fitting mercury abatement systems to all crematoria will need to be done to counteract this pollution.

Gold in teeth and jewellery is broken down so small that it cannot be found in the ashes. Other metals, such as those used in hip replacements or other orthopaedic surgeries, can be removed by a magnet. If permission is received from relatives, the metals are sent for recycling.

Crematoria across the UK work with Orthometals, a Dutch company that specialises in sorting and recycling metal remains after cremation. Some of the proceeds are returned to the crematorium, who may choose to donate the money to charity. In Plymouth, the metals are sent to a Cornish company for recycling, then any proceeds are sent to a local Lord Mayor's Charity. The recycling of metals from crematoria over the UK has raised well over £1 million for charity since it began in Britain in 2004.

Guidance for crematoria is now becoming more stringent, and monitoring of emissions is more rigorous, which will improve pollution in the future. If this is an issue for you then always check which of your local crematoria is the most environmentally friendly.

What Happens on the Day?

Family and friends will normally gather in the waiting room a few minutes before the ceremony time and will be met by the celebrant, who will have checked the music is correct beforehand. If you are using a funeral director, they will arrive with the hearse and principal mourners and the crematorium chapel attendant will accept the coffin by checking the name plate to ensure the correct identity.

When the celebrant and the principal mourners are ready to proceed, the coffin will be carried into the chapel by the funeral director or family bearers. The coffin will be placed on the catafalque (a stand to support the coffin), and everyone will be directed to their seats, ready for the ceremony to start.

At the end of the ceremony, there will be time for saying a last goodbye to your loved one and to follow the celebrant outside. Only then will the coffin be taken out of the chapel for cremation. The body will be cremated within seventy-two hours and the ashes will be available to collect after a few days.

There are many crematoria in my area; some of them are in cities but two are in country areas. Glynn Valley Crematorium in Cornwall is very special and shows that crematoria do not need to be stark. The view there is impressive and one day the ceremony came to a halt as, through the beautiful picture window, we watched a steam train cross the horizon. Another afternoon, the attention of the congregation was lost as they were all staring behind me. When I turned around they were watching a family of deer grazing in the meadow just outside the window.

Traditional Burials

At a burial, the funeral ceremony may take place at a church, chapel or crematorium but also at the graveside of your loved one. Burial is usually more expensive than cremation as, in addition to the interment fee, there may be other charges for grave maintenance.

The coffin is placed on slats and three straps are put in place as support. Once the committal has been said, family and friends may wish to place a flower each on the coffin to say goodbye. The bearers then come forward, hold the straps, and as the slats are removed, they gently lower the coffin into the grave. Traditionally, handfuls of earth are thrown onto the coffin, but you can also throw flower petals. The grave is not filled until people have left the burial site, unless the family want to take part. There has been a rise in graveside rituals in recent years, which include live music, firework displays, releasing balloons and doves, and even fly-pasts!

Jim

At Jim's burial, his family asked the local brass band to stand together and play one of Jim's favourite songs, 'Amazing Grace', as the coffin was lowered.

Natural Burial or Green Funeral

A natural burial returns a body to the earth in as natural a way as possible, generally involving biodegradable caskets or coffins such as cardboard, willow, wicker or bamboo. Non-embalming is required and the burial often takes place in green spaces such as wildflower meadows, protected woodland and parkland. Some natural burial sites are also privately owned farms, forests, land or meadows where you can be buried among, and contribute to, local wildlife.

Some burial grounds will let you mark the grave with a temporary wooden marker. Wild flowers, native to the area, can be planted on the grave and some allow trees to be planted to mark the spot. Always visit the ground beforehand and ask all your questions, e.g. your closest place may not plant trees, which may be a specific requirement for your loved one.

Natural burials can also be considerably less expensive than traditional burials and often play an important role in conservation efforts. When spaces are set up as natural burial grounds, they are protected from development and have a long-term future as a wild space in which nature is allowed to thrive. Some become successful woodlands and others become pastures for animals. Families can return year after year and watch the seasons change, connecting with wildlife and listening to the birds sing.

Erika

For a wild swimmer's ceremony, it was fitting that Erika's family and friends met at the natural burial ground overlooking the River Dart, and her best friend sang 'Moon River' as they said farewell. After the first verse everyone joined in and, as they raised their voices, a rainbow appeared over the river.

Burial at Sea

Anyone can be buried at sea, as long as the person arranging it has a licence from the Marine Management Organisation (www.gov.uk/guidance/how-to-get-a-licence-for-a-burial-at-sea-in-england). At the moment, there are only three designated burial sites in English coastal waters: Tynemouth, Tyne and Wear; Newhaven in East Sussex; and The Needles Spoil Ground near the Isle of Wight.

Harry

After spending World War Two in the Royal Navy, Harry had always wanted his body to be buried at sea. His family knew that it would take about five hours to reach the burial site in the boat and the sea would be quite choppy. Unfortunately, his family suffered from sea sickness so they chose to have a ceremony on land, before saying goodbye to Harry from the quayside.

Home Burial

It is legal to be buried on your property if you own it in its entirety. You do not need planning permission, but the person responsible must also be in possession of a certificate of authority for burial, create a simple burial register with a plan showing the exact location of the grave, and record the burial on the deeds.

There are certain restrictions, e.g. the plot needs to be far away from water supplies and only two bodies are allowed to be buried on the site. You need to keep the documentation safe, just in case you or your family sell your property in the future, as it will have to be included in the sales details. Bear in mind, though, that once the property is sold, family and friends cannot visit the grave without the new owner's permission.

Jean

Bill wanted to bury his beloved wife, Jean, in their garden. He even dug the grave himself. When his family arrived for the ceremony, Bill handed them all a glass of sherry, Jean's favourite drink, and they all shared their memories and stories of their wife, mum and grandmother, as they sat around her coffin. As her sons lowered the coffin into the grave, everyone placed Jean's favourite rose, Peace, onto the coffin.

After they had filled in the grave, they planted a tree: a crab apple that Jean had grown from a pip a few years ago and had now taken to blossoming beautifully in the spring. They all agreed it was the perfect end to Jean's happy life.

Future Trends

As time goes by, more and more eco-friendly end-of-life options are being developed.

A Swedish company, Promessa (www.promessa.se), have devised a way of freezing the body in liquid nitrogen then vibrating it until it reduces to dust. This is then placed in a coffin made of potato starch and maize for burial, which composts within a year.

The term 'Resomation' (www.resomation.com) is derived from the Greek or Latin word for 'rebirth of the human body'. It is a quieter and less environmentally damaging process, as instead of a traditional cremation using fire, this process uses water and an alkali-based solution to break down the body to produce ash, which is then returned to the family.

Composting allows you to choose an end-of-life option that strengthens the environment, rather than depleting it. Recompose (www.recompose.life), a company in the USA, place the body in a cradle surrounded by wood chips, alfalfa and straw, which is then laid into a vessel and covered with more plant material for thirty days as microbes break everything down, resulting in the formation of a nutrient-dense soil. This is then made available to relatives, who can spread it in their garden or use it to plant a tree.

2.3

The Coffin
and Transport

The journey doesn't end here.
Death is just another path, one that we all must take.

—J.R.R. Tolkien, *Lord of the Rings: The Return of the King*

Once you have decided where you will have the funeral, the next step is to discuss with your family about the coffin and transport to the ceremony.

Coffins

There are so many different choices available, depending on cost, materials and design. You can choose an environmentally friendly coffin – some even reflect the personality and taste of your loved one.

Traditional wooden coffins and caskets are made of oak or pine, but you can also choose cardboard coffins or veneered MDF. Coffins made of natural material such as wool, wicker, willow, bamboo, seagrass and banana leaves are also available. Some are suitable for cremation and others for burial, so check first.

If you have chosen an eco-friendly burial in a green burial site, a biodegradable coffin or casket is used, usually made out of recycled paper, wicker or willow.

Sea burials have very strict rules about the type of coffin you can use. It must be made from solid softwood and must not contain any plastic, lead, copper or zinc. This is to make sure it biodegrades and to protect the area from contamination.

Top Tip

If you wish to repatriate your loved one abroad, the coffin must be zinc-lined and the person must be embalmed. Always check the airline for extra regulations.

There is even a company in the Netherlands, Loop Biotech (www.loop-of-life.com), that makes coffins out of mycelium, a living fungus that naturally grows underground amongst the roots of trees, plants and fungi. Not only is it biodegradable but it also provides nutrients to the plants growing around it. It can also clean up soil by converting waste products into nutrients.

Personalised Coffins
The Kane Kwei Carpentry Workshop in Ghana is famous

for creating 'fantasy' coffins to celebrate a life at a funeral. The coffins are shaped and painted to reflect the hobbies, personality or career of the person who has died. For example, a fish-shaped coffin is a common request for a fisherman, or important leaders are often buried in a wooden lion.

In the UK, Creative Coffins in Essex (www. creativecoffins.co.uk) make environmentally friendly coffins in many designs, which can be personalised with extra details. The coffins are made from a mixture of recycled cardboard and paper and a requested design can be printed onto them using a collection of environmentally friendly inks. You can lie in a coffin that has been decorated to look like a box of chocolates, a cider bottle with your name on the front, or even depicting the Red Arrows if you didn't get to fly with them in your life.

If you want to decorate the coffin yourself, choose a wicker or cardboard coffin and ask your family to decorate it. Alternatively, you can buy a plywood flat-pack coffin from the Coffin Club (www.coffinclub.co.uk/product/chistann-coffin/) and assemble it yourself before decorating it.

Georgia

One artist I met, Georgia, kept her own coffin in her workshop and had just finished painting it with flowers before she died. She included her family and friends in the decorating process, adding photos, messages and poems that allowed them to express their feelings and help with their grief. On the day of her funeral, the coffin became the focal point, and family and friends were asked to write last-minute messages with felt-tip pen. Her family felt that instead of the coffin being hidden away it now represented love and joy.

Shrouds

Shrouds are an eco-friendly alternative to a coffin and have been used since ancient times. Bellacouche in Devon (www.bellacouche.com) offer a range of biodegradable wool felt eco-coffins and woollen shrouds for natural burial or cremation. You can make your own at one of their Cocoon workshops or buy online.

Transport

The journey to the crematorium or burial place is an emotional part of the service. You can choose from a traditional hearse or horse-drawn carriage through to a Land Rover or bus – in fact, any form of transport that reflects the life of the loved one. One family of a keen motorcyclist and banger racer chose a motorcycle hearse. There are also groups of motorcyclists who will follow the hearse in convoy, escorting the coffin to its final resting place.

Top Tip

You can hire a van or use your own car to transport the coffin; there are no restrictions as long as the transport has a good load length.

Ted

Ted's family arrived at the ceremony with their dad's coffin in their camper van, which represented all their family holidays over the years and the great fun they had together.

Procession

In the UK, a funeral procession comprises family and close friends following the coffin of their loved one as it is taken to its final resting place. Often the procession will pass important places in the life of their loved one, and together, family and friends can remember and celebrate. Friends and neighbours line the streets and either clap or remove their hats to show support for the family.

Funeral processions are not the same the world over but they serve the same purpose, showing respect and support from the wider community. Drawing on other cultures can make the funeral procession even more personal. A procession unique to the New Orleans, Louisiana and Cajun culture blends traditional European and African culture. A jazz band leads the deceased to the crematorium or burial place, playing dirges and sad music all the way. After the ceremony, the band plays uplifting music to celebrate the life of the deceased.

Top Tip

Make sure everyone knows what you have decided for the procession by placing a notice in the local paper or on social media with details of the time and route.

Ginny

Ginny had made many friends throughout her short life. When she died at only eighteen, they all wanted to be involved. As restrictions were in place due to Covid-19, her family were only allowed sixteen mourners at their local crematorium; however they contacted Ginny's friends through social media to let them know when she was going to be driven through the town centre, along the riverside and past Ginny's school.

On the day, Ginny's friends lined the route, all wearing clothes in Ginny's favourite colour, purple. As the hearse drove along the road, her friends clapped and cheered to say goodbye to their dearest friend and classmate.

Pallbearers

A pallbearer is one of up to six people (both men and women) who help to carry the coffin at a funeral at waist height, on their shoulders, or wheeled in with the assistance of a small trolley known as a wheel bier. Many families choose either family members or close friends of the deceased to carry the coffin, or the funeral director will provide their own bearers.

In Ghana, there is a group of pallbearers who have devised a flamboyant dance routine to give the deceased a joyous final send-off while bringing a little bit of happiness to those who are grieving. Benjamin Aidoo, the group's leader, wants to teach the world to hold joyful funerals, and is planning to expand his business across the globe. Ghanaian funerals are important social occasions and Benjamin always asks the bereaved family beforehand if they want to give their loved one a traditional funeral or a 'dancing trip' to heaven.

PART 3

The Funeral Ceremony

3.1

Funeral
Celebrants

I've learned that people will forget what you said,
people will forget what you did,
but people will never forget how you made them feel.

—Maya Angelou

What Does a Celebrant Do?

The dictionary definition of a celebrant is: 'a person who performs a rite'. This has traditionally meant a vicar, minister or priest, with the ceremony taking place in a church or other religious building. These days, we have more choices and the importance of selecting the right celebrant for your loved one's celebration of life cannot be underestimated.

The celebrant is there to hold the ceremony together and make sure it runs smoothly. They set the tone, cue the music and introduce the speakers. It is preferable to have someone who is not emotionally attached to the deceased, can speak well and will also deal with any unexpected occurrences. At a crematorium, the celebrant also has to make sure the ceremony keeps to time.

This is the one occasion when your loved one's life story is to be told, their memories are honoured and their body is put to rest. The celebrant will meet the family in advance and – through sensitive questioning and careful listening – enable them to have their stories and feelings shared, before writing the ceremony and reading it on the day. The family should choose someone they feel comfortable with.

To find a celebrant, recommendations from friends are helpful and online research is worth doing – always check the celebrant's testimonials. It is entirely your choice who leads the ceremony and, even though the funeral director may recommend a celebrant, check they are experienced, fully trained and aligned to your values and beliefs. Bear in mind that celebrants work *with* the funeral directors and are not employed by them.

Celebrant fees will be listed under 'prices on request' on the funeral director's website. This means that celebrants can continue to offer a completely personalised service at a cost that is appropriate to their creativity, experience and local economic market.

Top Tip

Check that the celebrant has a code of practice (www.iocf.org.uk/code-of-practice) or has adopted the Funeral Celebrant Accord devised by The Funeral

Celebrancy Council (www.funeralcelebrancycouncil. org.uk), a central organisation aimed at defining best practice for funeral celebrants across the UK.

Religious Celebrant

When a family is a member of a church, they may want to talk to their church minister. For families that do not belong to a church but would like a Christian funeral this can be arranged as well, as anyone is entitled to a Church of England funeral within the parish they live in.

Humanist Celebrant

Humanist celebrants are members of Humanists UK (www.humanism.org.uk) and are trained by them too. Humanists UK is an organisation of non-religious people who have a scientific view of the universe. They offer a secular or non-religious ceremony and have their own belief system, so do not include any religious or spiritual content in their ceremony.

Independent Celebrant

Independent celebrants (www.iocf.org.uk) offer freedom of choice, officiating funeral services with or without religion. There are so many ways of celebrating that include spiritual or religious elements as well as elements from your own faith and traditions, such as Buddhist, Pagan and spiritual beliefs. Independent celebrants can include prayers and hymns and perform a religious committal for cremation and burials.

Gregory

I have had ministers of all faiths attend my ceremonies, but one will always stay in my mind. Gregory had married Ada, a girl from Thailand, and at his funeral she wanted her Buddhist priest to perform the committal. He arrived in his glorious yellow robes and led the congregation in a chant, which included humming and ringing a bell. It was memorable as well as moving, and Ada was so pleased to have had her religion included.

Both types of celebrants (humanist and independent) are completely family-centred and can officiate natural, alternative or even themed funerals. They are there to support you, to be a hand to hold and to honour the memory of your loved one. Celebrants are also ritual experts who will think outside of the box to find old and new ways to celebrate and remember your loved one's life in a compassionate and caring manner.

It is important that, whoever you choose, the funeral ceremony reflects the wishes, beliefs and values of the deceased and their family and is respectful and highly personal. Remember that *you* decide who to lead the ceremony, not the funeral director.

A good celebrant will always offer you a presentation script after the funeral as a family keepsake. This can become part of the family resource, handed on to future generations as a chronicle of the times. It is a way of keeping ancestors alive and can be read for future generations.

3.2

———

Creating
the Ceremony

For a society to be healthy, people must significantly
mark the milestones of life through ceremony and ritual.

—Carl Jung

The aim of a funeral ceremony is to bring comfort
to the bereaved, as well as acknowledging the life of
the deceased with honour and respect. It is a time to
celebrate the life, journey and achievements of someone
who has made a lasting impact on those who knew them.
It is also a time to say farewell, in the way that best suits
those involved.

The ceremony is not just for your loved one but also
for the people left behind, as it can help with the grieving
process. A good ceremony is memorable and stays in
people's minds for a long time, making you appreciate
your own life and the lives of those closest to you.

The celebrant you choose will suggest meeting at a
venue where you are most comfortable, not in a public

place. You need to be somewhere private, where you will not be disturbed and where you and your family can express emotions without fear of upsetting others. Since Covid-19, meetings have taken place via Zoom, phone calls and WhatsApp.

Once everyone is present it is a good idea to turn off all distractions, such as the television or background music, then share a cup of tea together. Read out messages written on sympathy cards, and take the opportunity to share what your loved one means to each of you. Looking at photographs of your loved one can bring up many stories, and laughing along with each other's memories gives everyone the courage to keep sharing.

A healthy dose of humour not only helps us to cope more easily with everyday life but it also lifts us during particularly difficult and challenging times. The creator of the Muppets, Jim Henson's funeral was a happy send-off. Everyone was forbidden to wear black and Big Bird sang Kermit's signature song, 'It's Not Easy Being Green'. The ceremony ended with singing from the Muppet choir.

Asking the question, 'when were they happiest?' can bring forward memories of your loved one spending time in the garden, holidays abroad, being surrounded by family and even baking cakes for the Women's Institute.

A good, professional celebrant will be able to sensitively find out the essence and personality of your loved one and weave anecdotes and memories throughout the ceremony. They will also include any faiths and beliefs, rituals, cultural preferences and family traditions that are important to you all.

People often believe that a funeral ceremony should follow a set structure, and sometimes this can be a comfort to the family. There are elements common to a funeral ceremony that can be included, such as orders of service, eulogies and music, but the funeral ceremony should ideally reflect the life and personality of your loved one. The more unique and memorable you can make it, the more personal it will feel.

Order of Service

The first step is to decide the structure of the ceremony and create an order of service, which will guide family and friends through the ceremony and can also be kept afterwards. It can include the full name of the deceased with dates of birth and death, music choices, poems, donation details, and where and when the funeral is taking place. It does not include the eulogy, tribute or any of the other words from the ceremony.

A typical order of service layout can include the following:

- Entrance music
- Welcome and introduction
- Poems, prayers or readings
- Eulogy/tribute
- Reflective music
- Committal/farewell
- Closing words
- Exit music

You can send this layout on to the funeral director to print, along with photographs of your loved one. Alternatively, family and friends can design and print this themselves, making it a personal reflection of their loved one's life.

Astrid

For Astrid, an artist, her family made a booklet showing copies of her favourite paintings. They also included photographs from her early childhood to a recent holiday, and included group photos with her family. Her husband sent copies to family abroad who couldn't get to the funeral and the document is still discussed at family meetings.

Each part of the ceremony is there for a reason, so the following describes the purpose of each section.

Welcome and Introduction

This opening segment is for welcoming everyone to the ceremony, but it also mentions family and friends who cannot attend for any reason. It serves as an introduction and explains that the funeral ceremony is a way to say farewell, to show the affection and regard in which the loved one was held, and gives time to remember and celebrate the person that they were. It acknowledges the shared grief of family and friends which, in turn, creates invisible bonds that draw everyone closer together.

Music

Every ceremony is unique and personal, and music can be crucial in setting the tone and feel. Music can bring people together in emotionally distressing times and also give pointers back to the past, drawing on family traditions that have been laid down and maintained over the years. Hymns and religious music are sometimes chosen for this reason and it is always moving to see family and friends stand and sing a favourite hymn together.

Songs that have the most impact are often those that were favourites of the deceased because the lyrics and style reflected their life, loves and achievements. Music can also celebrate special events in their lives such as a first dance song or music chosen for their son's wedding. The music that you choose can be purely instrumental or with lyrics; it may be a live performance or pre-recorded. If your loved one enjoyed walking on the moors, maybe you could listen to a recording of birdsong?

Top Tip

To find out about your loved one's taste in music, begin by talking to family and friends and looking at their CD or record collection.

There could be a professional singer who will perform the music that has special meaning for your family, from sacred music and favourite hymns to popular songs.

Everyone can sing together – maybe a song that strongly resonates with the loved one's life and legacy and, ideally, is familiar to the majority of those present. The lyrics can be printed in the order of service so that everyone can follow the words as they sing together.

As the coffin enters the ceremony space, the music begins. Many families choose a quiet piece of music as everyone finds their seat and the ceremony starts. Part way through the ceremony, and before the committal or farewell, another piece of music can be played. This can be one of the deceased's – or the family's – favourite songs and is referred to as the reflective music. This is a time for each of the mourners to recall their own memories and to pray if they wish. At the end of the funeral an upbeat piece of music may be chosen as people leave the ceremony.

These days, funerals can be a celebration of a life well lived.

Betty
Betty's two daughters turned up at her funeral in fifties colourful vintage outfits and, at the end of the ceremony, danced back down the aisle to 'Chantilly Lace' by the Big Bopper.

Sometimes the music has been chosen by the loved one before they died.

Winnie
Winnie had a large family of seven grown-up children and many grandchildren, and she left instructions that they had to play air guitar to Queen's 'Bohemian

Rhapsody' at the end of her funeral ceremony. Her family all stood up self-consciously as the music began, then, when the volume was turned up, they threw themselves into the air guitar with gusto. Everyone stood up and joined in and, afterwards, an elderly lady at the back said it was the best funeral she had ever been to!

Music invokes strong emotions. Hear a piece of music from decades ago and you are transported back to that particular moment, like stepping into a time machine. You can feel everything as if you were actually there. Family and friends have been moved by slide shows of a person's life accompanied by a track of their favourite music.

Mick
'Rock Around the Clock' was played at Mick's ceremony as his children watched photos of their dad as a Teddy boy in the 1950s.

The ability to play and sing music can also be celebrated.

Paul
Paul was a talented musician and morris dancer. He had taught many dances at festivals all over the world throughout his life, always ending the sessions by singing songs from the English folk scene. At his funeral, his son and daughter played one of his favourite traditional morris tunes, 'Princess Royal', on the violin and guitar.

Our lives are full of music, whether we are aware of it or not, and TV and film themes feature strongly. *The Archers* theme is a very popular choice and may bring back memories of sitting all together by the radio after dinner.

Top Tip

There is no right or wrong choice of music, but the music selected by the family is always right!

Poems and Prayers

Bereavement is a complex emotion and is linked with a variety of rich traditions and customs to honour the deceased and comfort loved ones. These traditions vary greatly between religions, cultures and belief systems, and sometimes knowing the right things to say or do can be very challenging when struggling with emotions and comforting others. A family member or friend may choose a poem that they are happy to read rather than putting themselves through the pressure of reading a eulogy or tribute.

Choosing the right prayers and poems can help families process their grief in the most difficult of times, raising the spirits and calming the soul. Sometimes the deceased has left a poem that means a lot to them, but if this is not the case, a poem may be found that fits the person perfectly. The internet can play an important part in your research, but looking at poetry books and asking friends and family for recommendations may bring forward a poem that fits perfectly. Religious prayers are often requested and many funeral ceremonies include 'The Lord's Prayer'.

Eulogy/Tribute

The eulogy – sometimes called the tribute – is the biggest part of the ceremony as it tells the memories, stories and recollections of your loved one and what they meant to family and friends.

The eulogy can be written in different ways; the story can begin when they were born and include tales of their childhood and education, qualifications, first jobs and formative experiences. It can continue through other events such as marriage and children, and can include talents, hobbies and other interests. Contacting family and friends from all stages of their life will help discover more stories. Alternatively, memories from family and friends can be woven together as an overview of what this person meant to them.

John

What can we say about John? He loved his family a hundred per cent, protecting and supporting them with immense humour and dedication. He loved to drink iced gin and tonic and hated warm beer. He adored his comfy armchair and his dog, Susie, and, as a Yorkshire man, was wary of anyone from Lancashire. Through all the trials in his life he always tried to look on the bright side.

Another idea is to pick a theme to reflect how your loved one would like to be remembered, such as a song lyric or poem.

Ali

Ali had died from a drug overdose. The crematorium was full of her family and friends, but no one felt able to share her story. Her sister chose the song 'Human' by Rag 'n' Bone Man, as the lyrics said more than Ali's short history would convey:

It is a good idea to include any sayings your loved one was known for and what they were like as a person. This usually leads to a lively debate at family meetings, and phone calls are made to distant relatives to fill in the gaps. Sometimes you learn something about the person that you didn't already know. Family members and people who played an important part in their life can also be named and acknowledged.

At the ceremony, a family member can read the tribute or the celebrant will read it for them. Depending on time, there can also be a space for people to stand up and speak if they choose.

Top Tip

For a cremation, timing the ceremony is vital as there is a time limit in many crematoria. As an estimate, five hundred words takes about five minutes to read.

Committal and Farewell

The committal is an opportunity to offer one last farewell to your loved one. It is also a time to add formality to the occasion. The mourners will be asked to stand and the celebrant will face the coffin with some heartfelt words. Families have different views and may choose to have a poignant poem instead of personal words. They may feel that their loved one is being reunited with their spouse or parents. There's no wrong or right way; only what feels comfortable and appropriate.

Frank
Frank was a Spiritualist and believed in life after death.
His daughter chose these words for his committal:

> *We now commit Frank's body to be reunited with his beloved wife, Sheila. His family take comfort they are now back together and will remain so for eternity.*
>
> *Frank's journey is just beginning, but there is also grief, loss and pain. Everyone here has had their life touched; perhaps in the smallest way, or perhaps even transformed by Frank's existence. His life mattered.*

Closing the Curtains

If the ceremony is in a crematorium, it is your choice whether the curtains close at the end of the committal, and for some families this remains the preferred option. Closing the curtains can be seen as a symbol of letting the person go and a final farewell.

Music can be softly played, or even soundtracks that are more personal to your loved one, such as the sound of a steam train leaving the station or birdsong for nature lovers.

Some families feel this is too painful, and so the curtains can then be closed at the end of the ceremony, or not at all, especially if family would like to go up to the coffin at the end to say their personal farewells or lay a flower. Always remember that it is your choice.

Closing Words

After the committal, the closing words are a way of summing up the person's character and beliefs. At the end of the ceremony it is important for family and friends to be uplifted and to have hope for the future.

The closing words are also a way of sharing their legacy. Everyone leaves something behind when they die: a child, a recipe, a garden planted. Sometimes they leave behind a legacy of not just practical skills but a way of living that has had an impact on all who met them. This legacy may be a wealth of memories, leaving your loved one remembered as a living, vital presence who has truly made a difference to the world.

It is good to know that we no longer need to be confined to a traditional religious service, especially if we have different beliefs. In the end, a great way to honour your loved one's life is by celebrating who they were as an individual by personalising their celebration. With a little imagination, you can create a one-of-a-kind celebration that would not only put a smile on their family and friends' faces, but probably produce a few laughs as well.

Memorial Ceremony

There are many reasons why a memorial ceremony is chosen to celebrate and honour a person's life. There may be no actual physical body to bury if your loved one has chosen to donate their body to science. Other circumstances may be due to a death as a result of a natural disaster, car accident or disappearance.

You may have chosen to have a direct cremation or a small, private burial. A memorial ceremony gives families the freedom and flexibility to hold a ceremony wherever and whenever they like, maybe on a special anniversary or the person's birthday.

Holding a memorial ceremony at one of your loved one's favourite places, such as a park, village hall, beach, restaurant or even your own home, reduces the stress of time constraints in a more formal setting. You can arrange a special afternoon tea or dinner and invite family and friends when they are all available. As there is no coffin, a memory table could be set up as a focus for the ceremony instead. This can include items such as artwork, awards, medals, pictures, sporting equipment, books… anything that meant a lot to the deceased. You can even include large items such as their motorcycle or car, or a sculpture.

A memorial ceremony can be a very uplifting and heart-warming event when friends and family are sharing their stories of how the individual had impacted them. It can also serve as a means of closure, helping family and friends to accept and deal with their loss and continue on with their lives.

Memorial Websites

Much Loved (www.muchloved.com) is a memorial website enabling you to share memories, tributes and stories of your loved one with family and friends. This not-for-profit charity was set up to help families with bereavement and they do not charge for their services. The website also has sections on donations, funeral notices and photographs.

Personalising Funerals

Weep if you must, parting is hell,
But life goes on, so sing as well.

—Joyce Grenfell

The most meaningful funeral captures the life and personality of the person, which can be shown through the choice of music, poems and flowers and the involvement of family and friends. Over a person's life, they may have shared their journey with many people; friendships have been made, love shared and memories created. Adding personal touches to their funeral can involve all these people who meant so much to them. Here are some ideas to consider when adding a personal touch to a funeral.

Favourite Colours

Some people believe that it is mandatory to wear black at a funeral to show respect, but it has not always been so. Even though Victorians wore black, as mourning went on the colour lightened to grey, mauve and white. Before Queen Victoria died in 1901, she left very detailed instructions for her funeral. Not only did she wear her white wedding veil over her face, she also requested white horses and a white pall over her coffin to be part of her send-off.

It may be the wish of the person who has died for mourners to wear bright colours, or the family may ask to wear a specific colour or ribbon in support of a charity.

Dave
Dave's family wanted everyone to wear Manchester United colours. They draped their grandad's Manchester United scarf on his coffin and then sang 'Glory Glory Man United' at the end.

Gail
Gail's family decided to honour their sister's memory by wearing her favourite footwear, Crocs, in bright colours.

Coffin Drape

A coffin drape is a piece of material to place over the coffin that tells the story of the deceased. Family and friends can write words, draw pictures and attach photos and poems that reflect their loved one's interests and life story.

Alison

As their mother was a keen seamstress, Alison's family made a patchwork coffin drape using their mother's clothes she had kept over the years. At the funeral, everyone came forward to stand around the coffin and the history of each patchwork piece was discussed.

The drape can go with the deceased, but many families take them home and hang them in pride of place.

Personal Items

Celebrating a life by showcasing the person's talents makes the ceremony even more personal. Families can bring in paintings, pottery or woodwork; in fact, anything that their loved one has treasured over the years. Families also like to reflect their loved one's jobs by placing items such as military caps or medals on their coffin.

Trevor

For a local dustbin man, Trevor, his family had made a cardboard dustbin lorry and placed it, along with a bottle of brandy, on his coffin. The ceremony closed with 'My Old Man's a Dustman', and we laughed at the story that, every Christmas, he would collect all the glasses of brandy his customers would give him, pouring them into a large bottle to drink at home. The resulting cocktail must have been very potent!

Fred

When Fred, a Cornish miner, died, his family contacted a local mining museum to source the miners' equipment. A miner's lamp was carried during the procession, and the coffin had a pair of pit boots and a helmet displayed on top.

Bernard

At Bernard's funeral, the family arrived and placed an extremely tatty bag on top of the coffin. This was Bernard's holiday bag, and he always took it with him. It went with him on his last journey, together with his passport, as they sang 'Wish Me Luck as You Wave Me Goodbye'.

Prem

Prem had a special interest in feathers. She would pick up feathers on her many long walks as she believed they were sent to her as messages from angels. Her family tied pink ribbons to her feathers and everyone at her ceremony was asked to bring their feathers to the front and place them in a basket to say goodbye. The basket full of feathers was then placed on the coffin as the committal words were spoken.

Families can create a memory table to display favourite photos, medals and certificates, and items that reflect the life their loved one led.

Patrick

Patrick's life was represented on the memory table beside his coffin, which included his fiddle, camera, walking boots, bee suit, wet suit, photographs (including a Himalayan photo) and a book of his favourite poetry.

Gabriel
At Gabriel's funeral, there were tags and a pen on each seat. Everyone wrote their wishes and messages for Gabriel on the tags and tied them onto the coffin. Guests were also asked to write messages in a memory book, which was kept by the family to read later.

It was traditional for the Maya in Latin America to bury their dead with maize in their mouths as a symbol of rebirth. Grave goods like food, jade, whistles and statuettes were provided to guide the dead through the afterlife. In the UK, you can usually place any objects inside, or on, a coffin that is going to be buried in a traditional grave. Did you know that the author Roald Dahl was buried with his favourite items, which included snooker cues, chocolate and a bottle of Burgundy?

Betty
Betty had asked to be buried with a small bell as a signalling device, just in case she was buried alive.

If the body is to be cremated, items such as wooden rosary beads, flowers, soft toys and written messages can also be placed inside the coffin. You cannot put in anything combustible such as a bottle of spirits, or certain materials including treated leather, latex and vinyl, as they create harmful emissions. Of course, you could drink the gin yourself before the cremation!

Candles

Lighting candles at funerals can be traced back to the early fourth and fifth centuries. The Macedonians would light candles for up to forty days after a death, believing the flame was a way to ward off ghosts and demons. The Greeks and Romans also used candles or torches as a way to guide the dead on their final journey.

The ritual of lighting a candle to pay tribute to a life has long been a part of our culture as well. Candles are a beautiful, natural way to bring the symbolism of everlasting life into a funeral service. We light candles as a sign of hope and comfort, and as a reminder of the light a loved one brought into our lives. They symbolise removing darkness and shining the light of wisdom, and are lit in the knowledge that the loved one's light will always shine and that death does not extinguish it.

James

At James's ceremony, everyone was given a nightlight in a glass jar, which they lit at a given signal. When the overhead lights were turned off, the committal was performed to flickering candlelight. The family asked everyone to take the candle with them and light it in remembrance on James's birthday.

Flowers

The traditional language of flowers provides a way to convey your feelings at a funeral. Bouquets of white lilies symbolise purity and sympathy; gladioli embody strength of character, sincerity and moral integrity; carnations evoke admiration and remembrance.

Roses can be a beautiful part of an arrangement of funeral flowers. Each colour symbolises a different emotion, such as innocence, love or courage. Yellow roses given by friends of the deceased symbolise their strong ties. When you include a single rose in a bouquet it expresses enduring love for the deceased.

Bright yellow spring tulips and daffodils are a symbol of renewal and fresh starts, to bring encouragement and hope to a person who is grieving or unhappy.

Popular flower tributes are usually made from chrysanthemums, with other flowers intertwined, and can spell out the name of your loved one. 'Dad' and 'Mum' are popular tributes, as well as the loved one's name.

Wendy
Wendy's family designed a tribute for a lady who was always smiling – 'Laughing Gran'!

As part of the ceremony, family and friends can come up and place a flower on the coffin to say goodbye. The flowers may have been their loved one's favourite or they could weave rosemary, for remembrance, through the handles of a wicker coffin.

Sylvia
Sylvia's family placed wildflowers and greenery from their local woodland, as their mum had always loved

walking there, as they listened to 'The Lark Ascending',
composed by Ralph Vaughan Williams.

Jessie
Poppies had always been a favourite of Jessie, as her
life's passion was telling the stories of soldiers from
both world wars through books and articles. Her
cardboard coffin was painted with poppies and her
family handed sachets of poppy seeds out to everyone
after the ceremony. As 'The Last Post' was played, every
family member placed a poppy on the coffin and said
their goodbyes. It was an emotional end to a beautiful
ceremony.

Recordings

People have been recording their voices since 1877, when
Thomas Edison invented the phonograph. It is becoming
popular to hear music played or sung by the deceased at
their own funeral.

Phyllis
Phyllis's family wrote their eulogy interspersed with
their mother's own singing and playing from amateur
dramatics shows.

Katrina
Katrina had been a jazz singer on cruise ships and her
sons had copied her tapes onto CDs for her to listen to
in the hospice. We listened to these recordings of her

warm, youthful voice as we watched photos of her life appear on a big screen, to many people's amazement as she had kept her early life a secret from her friends and neighbours.

Sean
At Sean's funeral, we listened to a recording of a lively Irish tune he had played on his fiddle.

Many of us have favourite radio and TV programmes that bring joy to us over the years. Humour plays a large part in many people's lives, and families love to hear recordings of 'The Blood Donor' by Tony Hancock or an extract from 'The Goon Show' that reminds them of their loved one.

Daniel
In Dublin, Daniel had a dying wish that had his family and friends laughing at his funeral. He had recorded his voice pretending to be trapped inside his coffin and is heard knocking frantically, trying to get out. Coming from a speaker on the ground, his voice boomed from his grave: 'Hello, hello, hello… let me out!'

Decorating Graves

Since the time of the Neanderthals we have decorated the gravesites of our dead. The Terracotta Army, the Taj Mahal and the pyramids are all elaborate forms of funerary art.

In ancient times, Norsemen erected rune stones in memory of the dead. These tall stones were carved with exquisite and intricate runes telling of the deceased's deeds. It is a Jewish tradition of placing small stones on a grave that goes back to a time when gravestones were not used; instead, small stones were piled to mark a grave. As long as visitors tended the grave and left stones, the dead would be remembered.

In a small town in Alaska, traditions have mixed with Christian beliefs. After someone dies, the family will erect a spirit house. These fantastic spirit houses, each about the size of a large doll's house, cover their body and are painted in the family's colours. According to native beliefs, everything taken from the earth must be allowed to return to it. Therefore the spirit houses are not maintained or repainted, but are allowed to crumble and become part of nature again.

Top Tip

It is worth checking at the burial site before decorating a grave. Many burial sites do not allow plastic but encourage natural wreaths and real plants and flowers.

Gifts and Favours

Giving gifts or funeral favours at the end of the ceremony is a way of saying thank you for the support of friends and family, and can act as a physical reminder of the loved one who has died. They can express thanks, help with remembrance, pay tribute, provide an outlet for grief or even offer a chance to smile for those who attend the funeral ceremony.

Paper hearts containing forget-me-not seeds can be handed out at the end of the ceremony. The hearts are then planted so that, year after year, the flowers will blossom; a heartfelt and long-lasting reminder of the person who has died.

Nancy
Nancy's family handed out bunches of daffodils to their guests, as they were her favourite flower.

Julie
Julie had been a talented baker and her family loved the idea of making colourful cupcakes to hand to everyone at the end of the ceremony.

Derek
Derek's family provided their father's homemade wine to drink as a toast at the graveside.

Jean
Jean had collected fridge magnets throughout her travels. Her family had placed a basket full of her magnets by the door so that family and friends could choose one in memory of Jean.

Roisin
Roisin had been very proud of her Irish heritage and

her family provided pewter shamrock charms attached
to a label printed with an Irish blessing:

> *May the road rise up to meet you,*
> *May the wind be always at your back,*
> *May the sun shine warm upon your face,*
> *May the rains fall softly upon your fields,*
> *And, until we meet again,*
> *May God hold you in the palm of His hand.*

Harriet
Harriet's friends handed out pebbles with her name
written in silver pen, with the instructions to place
them in the garden or potted plants, or to keep them in
their pocket as a reminder of Harriet's beachcombing
hobby.

Jacob
Jacob owned a tree nursery. When his dad died, Jacob
planted evergreen seedlings in small pots and presented
them to all his dad's friends at the end of the funeral.

There are so many ways to personalise a funeral, so it is important to start thinking about your funeral now and write your own wishes (see Section 5.2 Funeral Wishes). You can use the My Plan section (see Part 6) to jot down your notes and ideas. Hand your wishes to your loved ones so they know exactly what you want. Decide how you would like your funeral to be personalised and even make a recording of your voice, leaving messages for them all.

Top Tip

There is no right or wrong way to celebrate someone's life, so do whatever is right for you all.

3.4

What to Do
With the Ashes

Take me to some high place of heather, rock and ling,
Scatter my dust and ashes, feed me to the wind,
So that I will be part of all you see, the air you are breathing.

—**Ewan MacColl, 'The Joy of Living'**

There are many reasons why ashes are scattered or interred (buried). Sometimes it is because of cultural beliefs, for example in the Hindu culture the act of scattering is a way of freeing the soul or spirit. The ashes must be cast into a river, ideally the Ganges, and the mourners should then depart without looking back. Many people, though, believe that scattering ashes represents an environmental choice, freeing up land that would be traditionally used as a burial site.

When you cast your loved one's ashes over the earth or into the sea, you are creating a special place of memory but also letting them go and expressing and working through your grief.

There are strict regulations regarding identification of ashes throughout the whole of the cremation process, ensuring the ashes you collect are only from your loved one and not mixed with anyone else's.

When you do collect your loved one's ashes, the question is: what do we do with them now? Some people keep their parents' ashes on their mantlepiece for years, and when they dust say 'sorry to disturb you', then give them a kiss. Others leave the ashes with the funeral director and never pick them up. Any unclaimed ashes must be stored for at least five years, with efforts made by the funeral company to locate the rightful recipient, before they dispose of them in a garden of remembrance.

Nowadays, there are much more exciting ways to give your loved ones a good send-off.

Air and Space

Ashes can be scattered high above the countryside in a hot-air balloon or drone. There are even services that will release ashes as part of a tandem skydive or from a radio-controlled helicopter.

If your loved one would like their ashes to be scattered in space, you can opt for a space burial service that carries their ashes in a bespoke vessel to 100,000 feet (30 km) above the earth. They are then released into the stratosphere, travelling for many months and spreading out across the planet before ultimately returning to earth in undetectable traces in rainfall or snowflakes.

You can even choose to send the departed's ashes up

in a rocket, then have a wild firework display with all the family below eating fish and chips and sipping champagne!

Whatever you decide to do with the ashes, be aware of the wind direction.

Alan
When one family scattered their dad's ashes, they climbed to the summit of a mountain, said a few words and opened the urn. The wind blew the ashes back at them and they ended up coughing and spluttering. They all agreed that their dad, Alan, would have found this very funny!

Land

If you decide to inter the ashes on private land you will need the owner's permission first. For public parks you will need to contact the district or unitary authority parks department. On common land, like village greens or other beauty spots, it is encouraged that only small amounts of ashes are discretely scattered or interred off the beaten track.

Often, families choose a sports venue in memory of their loved one. Each club has their own rules and, sadly, many do not allow the scattering of ashes any more. Manchester City, however, has a memorial garden at the stadium, created by volunteers, including staff at the club and local businesses. They encourage families of fans to spread ashes and take time to remember.

Top Tip

Make sure you research where the ashes can be placed and obtain permission, if required.

Maurice
Maurice's family chose a local golf course and obtained permission. A year later they realised that, as they were not members, they couldn't revisit the site to pay their respects.

Long Barrows

Not only can you inter the ashes in the ground but also in the new long barrows that are now being built.

The Long Barrow at All Cannings, near Devizes in the UK (www.thelongbarrow.com) was the first 'Neolithic' long barrow to be built in the UK for 5,500 years. It was built in 2014, in the same traditional style, to be a place where cremated remains in urns are to be kept. Inside the chalk mound there are five chambers arranged off the passageway and niches have been built into the traditional handcrafted limestone walls, holding up to six urns.

The barrow is aligned to the sunrise of the winter solstice on 21 December when the sun will illuminate the internal stone passageway. It is a spiritual place where people of any or no faith can come to remember and give thanks for the lives of their loved ones. New barrows are now being built all over the UK, including one on the borders of Oxford, Northamptonshire and Warwickshire called the Mid-England Barrow.

Eco-Friendly Planting

To plant the ashes into a tree, first choose a biodegradable urn (www.urnsforashes.co.uk/urns/biodegradable-urns). Pick your seed – maple, beech, gingko, ash or pine – and fill the lower capsule with the ashes. Mix with the compost in the upper capsule and plant it. As the tree grows, the biodegradable capsule becomes part of the earth and the result is a beautiful tree in your loved one's memory.

Water

If your loved one spent happy times at the coast, choose their favourite hour of the day (maybe sunrise or sunset) and a sandy beach. Find a spot below the high tide line and use a gardening hoe or stick to carve a shape or symbol in the sand, such as a heart shape or your loved one's initials. Sprinkle the ashes into the trench, cover if you wish and wait until the tide washes the ashes away.

Susie
Susie came all the way from Australia so that her mum and nan could be scattered in their favourite holiday town: Brixham, Devon. Susie carried the ashes from Australia in two scatter tubes so that they could be

scanned and kept easily on board the plane. She needed to have a special certificate to carry the ashes on the plane.

After a lot of research into suitable places, they agreed on a beautiful park in Brixham, overlooking the harbour. As the ceremony was read, Susie scattered the ashes in two interlocking hearts under the oak tree. She listened to the seagulls and watched the boats in the harbour bob up and down. She was so moved that she wanted the same ceremony when her time came.

Top Tip

Save some of your loved one's ashes for a keepsake.

In Florida, USA, the ashes of the dead can be mixed with an eco-concrete material and then shaped into a reef ball and lowered into the ocean, where marine life and coral reefs will take root.

Rivers, lakes and canals are also a popular choice. There are even water urns available that will float for a while as goodbyes are said, then sink and break down naturally over time.

Personal Items

Since there is such limited space for burials in South Korea, they are creative with the bodies of their deceased. The body is cremated and pressed into jewellery-like beads, which are often colourful and can be kept in an urn or bottle.

Scattering Ashes, based in Devon, has a website (www.scattering-ashes.co.uk) full of ideas to turn ashes into keepsakes, including beads, rings, pendants, glass sculptures and even Christmas baubles. Having the keepsake near you ensures your memories are always safe, making a beautiful and personal memorial.

For a garden lover, you can house the cremated ashes in a garden sculpture, such as a bird bath or even a sundial.

Anik
Gerald chose a bird bath made out of Devon limestone for his wife Anik's ashes. As it is portable, it has gone with the family every time they have moved house.

PART 4

Specialised
Ceremonies

4.1

Babies and
Young People

We cannot judge a song by its duration
Nor by the number of its notes
We must judge it by the way it touches and lifts our souls
Sometimes those unfinished are among the most beautiful.

—**Anon**

Babies and Children

Funerals for children are especially hard for families, and nothing can soften the blow when faced with the shock of the death of a baby or child. There is great pain and deep sorrow, leaving families shocked and confused, wondering how they will ever come to terms with what has happened. Even though they will never fully recover, parents and family members may take comfort in a personal ceremony that describes their child and all the love that surrounded them.

Whatever choices you make are the right ones. You may want to dress your baby in a particular outfit and put special items in their coffin such as a soft toy, letter or photo. Family members may draw a picture or write a poem to place by your baby's side.

Charities such as Cherished Gowns UK (www.cherishedgowns.org.uk), provide the families of babies that are stillborn, miscarried or have died soon after birth with gowns and other items of clothing for their funerals. They use donated wedding dresses to make the gowns, hats, bootees, blankets and cloth nappies, and the service is completely free of charge. Each gown is sewn to perfectly fit the baby and gives parents the chance to say goodbye to their child in something special and beautiful.

If you have kept your baby at home, you can transport them to the funeral in your own car, or ask the funeral director to do this as they may have a car specially adapted for a small coffin.

Take your time to discuss what you would like for the ceremony. You can hold the coffin in your arms throughout the ceremony and ask your family and friends to surround you, rather than sit in the pews. You can choose your favourite music, poems, order of service and flowers. You can even let people know what colours you would like them to wear.

You may choose to have a ceremony at the crematorium or church with all your family and friends present or a private ceremony at home for just a few important people. Sometimes the parents are the only ones at the ceremony and they support each other while they listen to quiet music and say a prayer. The choice is yours.

Top Tip

Some parents have photographs taken at the ceremony, providing precious mementoes. These photos may be helpful for sharing with younger brothers and sisters as they grow older.

The following stories are from real ceremonies to give inspiration and to encourage you to personalise your little one's funeral:

Jessica

Jessica's parents asked everyone to bring a teddy bear on the day, which would then be donated to a local children's charity. Everyone sang nursery rhymes, listened to music, lit candles, and released doves and balloons after the ceremony.

Lily-Jane

Lily-Jane died when she was only ten and her whole family took part in the ceremony. They had decorated the small coffin with hearts and angels and each family member had written a letter to her and placed it by her side. Her school friends formed a guard of honour as Lily-Jane was carried into the crematorium. Everyone recorded their names in a memory book, along with a story or a particular memory they had of Lily-Jane and, as they listened to her favourite song, they passed the memory book around to capture as many memories as possible.

Max

When his family found out that four-year-old Max's illness would end in death, they talked about doing everything to keep him alive for as long as possible. Over time, though, they lovingly changed their position. They planned his funeral ceremony, fundraised by walking huge distances to help charities and were able to enhance Max's remaining days with laughter and love. The hearse at his funeral was led by motorbikes from the south-west of the UK, filling the air with the roar of engines. These large men then joined the ceremony with their helmets under their arms to show their respect.

Young People

It is difficult to understand the reasons why someone in the prime of their life dies. Families ask whether there must be some purpose for the early death of a loved one and, of course, there simply are no answers, however hard we look. You can, though, celebrate the fact that you have known them, though they are no longer with you, and you can celebrate that you were privileged and honoured to have been a part of their life. By focussing on their life, not their death, you truly do justice to all that they meant to their family and friends.

There is a poem that says:

Some are bound to die young.
By dying young a person stays young in people's memory.

If he burns brightly before he dies, his brightness shines for all time.

—Aleksandr Solzhenitsyn

The following stories give ideas on how you can celebrate your loved one's life and may invoke ideas of your own.

Bobby

Bobby had special needs and lived in a supportive home near to his family. He died on his fifteenth birthday in his sleep, and his funeral was attended by so many family and friends. Everyone was welcomed with the words: 'Bobby was a fisherman of life – and some of his catch are here today.'

His cheeky smile and caring way had left an imprint on all their lives, leaving behind plenty of memories to cherish. His father wanted everyone to celebrate the life of his son; a very special person, a beacon whose light would shine on forever in each and every one he met.

As ABBA was his favourite band – in fact, the only music he ever listened to – his family had chosen 'Super Trouper' and 'Knowing Me, Knowing You'. The ceremony ended with 'Thank You For the Music', as everyone joined in with the chorus.

Kat

The family of a young mother, Kat, who had died of a brain tumour, wanted her friends and family to celebrate her short life as fully as possible and also to include her four children. It was fitting that the stars were shining brightly that evening, as Kat had adored them, and her children carried paper stars into the ceremony and placed them on her coffin.

All her friends had written words to describe what she had meant to them and how she had made such a difference in their lives. Her husband, John, had written a love letter to his beloved wife to describe her strength of character, sense of humour, warmth and kindness. He lit a candle at the beginning of the ceremony and Kat's children released balloons at the end and watched them rise into the night sky.

There was no doubt that Kat's brightness would always shine for her family and friends, and her ceremony was a mixture of laughter and sadness.

James

The death of James in a car accident shocked and devastated everyone who loved him. He was only nineteeb years old and was popular in the small Cornish town where he had lived all his short life.

His father, who worked as a carpenter, decided to honour James by building his son's coffin himself. He chose elm, associated with the cycle of life, death and rebirth, and asked James's brothers to help him. All of James's family and friends contributed to the funeral ceremony; choosing music, readings and poems from his Cornish and Scottish background and decorating the town hall with photographs of James.

On the day, his family carried his coffin into the hall, packed with everyone who knew and loved him, and placed James on a table at the front as a local sea shanty group sang 'The Farewell Shanty'.

As videos and a slideshow of photographs from James's life were projected behind the coffin, friends and family stood up to speak about the impact James had made on them. Everyone was encouraged to tell stories and share memories and funny incidents about him. The applause was loud and there was a lot of laughter.

James's mum then led everyone as they tied coloured ribbons onto the coffin, before lighting nightlights in glass jars that family and friends had brought with them. The lights in the hall were turned off and I said the committal words as the flickering candles lit the room. We stood in silence for a minute then I asked everyone to raise their glass in a toast to James, a much-loved son, brother, grandson, boyfriend and friend, and a very much missed member of the whole community.

James's best friends then carried the coffin into a small side room for people to say their private goodbyes as the lights were turned on again and food and drink were served. James was then taken to the crematorium for a ceremony with his close family.

Two months later, everyone was invited to a memorial ceremony in a local woodland. His parents planted an oak tree and all the ribbons from the coffin were tied to the branches. James's ashes were scattered at the base of the tree and his family planted crocus bulbs, as a family friend sang 'Somewhere Over the Rainbow', unaccompanied. Since that day, the tree has become the centre of family and social events and is a fitting tribute to their beloved James.

4.2

———

Military Ceremonies

So take your place of honour
Among those who have gone before
And know you will be remembered
For now and evermore

—**Robert Longley**

Military funerals are a way of paying respect to men and women who have died in active service. Funerals that honour people who have served their country but have since left the armed forces are called 'veterans' funerals'.

In the UK there are ceremonial traditions for each of the armed services, so research is vital to find out whether they served with the Royal Navy, Army or Royal Air Force, which regiment they served in and any traditions that are important to them.

The Royal British Legion (www.britishlegion.org.uk) are able to give advice and provide help with arranging military rites for funerals. They can also provide contacts for those in the local area and community who might want to be a part of the funeral service of ex-Forces personnel.

A wreath supplied by the Royal British Legion or their parent regiment can be laid on the coffin. The person's medals can be displayed on their coffin, as well as their beret or service cap, and the correct service or regimental flag can be draped over their coffin. At the end of the funeral it is traditional for the flag to be folded and presented to loved ones. The local Royal British Legion or Regimental Association could be asked to carry the coffin and they may also send a standard (flag) bearer to the service.

One of the most recognisable traditions at British Armed Forces funerals is a ceremonial move called 'reversed arms'. This is performed during the funeral procession and sees the coffin's escort reversing their weapons – holding them underneath their arms, facing backwards. This is followed by a command to 'rest on your arms reversed', when guns are lowered and heads are bowed in a gesture of honour and respect.

When a member of the Royal Navy dies it is known as 'crossing the bar', and a Navy funeral could include a burial at sea. The Royal Navy also suggests that it's appropriate for ex-services personnel to use the Union Flag. The White Ensign should only be used for sailors who died in active service.

Top Tip

Each service and regiment have their own unique 'signature tunes'. For a former Royal Navy veteran, playing 'Hearts of Oak' at the end the ceremony would be a perfect choice.

When the deceased was a veteran who had served in the armed forces, their family may want to acknowledge their service by having a bugler perform 'The Last Post', followed by 'The Rouse' or 'Reveille' – a shorter bugle call that was used to call soldiers to their duties.

Alan

Alan was a Veteran of the Royal Welsh Fusiliers, so his family chose to play a recording of the Regimental March, 'Men of Harlech', as they walked into the crematorium.

Alan was proud to have served his country; he was in the Second Battalion and took part in the invasion of Madagascar in 1942. He also served in India and Burma during 1943–45, so his family knew it was absolutely right that Alan was being honoured with a military guard.

Alan's son read this next poem in memory of his beloved dad:

Why
Far above the storm clouds gathering
Far above that midnight sky

Looking out just past the rainbow
Where eagles dare not fly
Out among the ashes
Of heroes long since past
I will take my place among them
When that final die is cast
Let not your heart be troubled
That's what I've always heard
But I stood for what I believed in
With these my final words
For in this life but few things matter
In this short time that we have here
Leaving nothing behind but our honour
The thing we hold most dear

—Anon

After the committal words, the following poem was read in memory of all Alan's friends and comrades who had died in the war:

They shall not grow old, as we that are left
grow old,
Age shall not weary them, nor the years
condemn.
At the going down of the sun, and in the
morning,
We will remember them.

—Laurence Binyon, 'For the Fallen'

Alan's family and friends responded: 'We will remember them.'

As the bugler played 'The Last Post', the Standard Bearer dipped the flag, which returned upright as 'Reveille' was played. At the end of the ceremony, the Standard Bearer led the family out.

4.3

Difficult Funerals

Grief is the price we pay for love.

—**Queen Elizabeth II**

Suicide

It is difficult to understand the reasons why someone decides to take their own life, and you may be left with feelings of anger, guilt, helplessness and rejection. Added to that burden is the stigma, which can keep those left behind feeling isolated and unable to ask for much-needed support. You will have questions to which you will never know the answers.

Each family member had a different relationship with the person who died, and everyone grieves in their own way and at their own pace. However, talking about the bereavement can bring a family together to share their pain and give each other comfort and support.

There are a number of charities such as Suicide Bereavement UK (www.suicidebereavementuk.com) who will listen and understand that it helps to talk about what has happened. For many people, it will be the first chance that they have had to openly talk about what they are experiencing and feeling. Hearing how other people are coping with the aftermath of losing a loved one to suicide can help those who could be at risk of suicide themselves to feel more hopeful about their own life and future.

Male suicide has become the single biggest killer of men under the age of forty-five. Tom Chapman, a barber from Torquay, Devon, believes that the barbershop is a safe place for men to talk, so he founded The Lions Barber Collective (www.thelionsbarbercollective.com) in 2015. Since then, The Lions Barber Collective has developed to become a group of international barbers who campaign for the awareness of mental well-being and suicide prevention.

Tom says, 'Since starting The Lions Barber Collective, I have had a huge increase in men opening up and offloading while sat in the chair. I think giving them the green light to talk is what is most important. It is something that we can all do, with little or no training – just let people know that you're willing to listen with empathy and without judgement.'

Funerals for suicide victims can be some of the most difficult for families to arrange. Most suicides are unexpected, so no arrangements have been planned. Understandably, you may not be as comfortable with words and phrases that point towards a celebration of their life, so it is important to discuss the funeral ceremony of your loved one with family and friends and choose whether to call it a celebration of life, a ceremony of thanksgiving for their life, or a ceremony in memory of your loved one.

There is, however, something to celebrate. You can celebrate the fact that you have known them, though they are no longer here. You can celebrate that you were privileged and honoured to have shared your life with them.

Murder

When a death is due to murder, it is unbelievable, unexpected, tragic and a crime, all at once. You may feel that the loss of your loved one could have been avoided and it may stun you into a confusion of emotions, part of which may be feelings of guilt that you didn't do enough to help and protect your loved one. There may be times when the anger and pain seem too great and times when you feel your life is out of your control.

Being with other people who knew them may be a comfort to you and give you strength in the days ahead but, if they are also struggling with their grief, there are other people who will listen and help. Victim Support (www.victimsupport.org.uk) are independent of the police but work closely with them by offering the family a caseworker who will coordinate support. They can offer practical help such as dealing with phone calls, letters and helping with funeral arrangements. They can also help with claiming compensation and provide information about the police, coroner, and other parts of the criminal justice system that become involved after a homicide.

It can often be very difficult for families when there is a delay in the release of the body of their loved one from the coroner's office before a funeral can take place. This delay could be used to decide how the funeral ceremony would best honour their loved one. They may have had strong wishes and beliefs about being cremated or buried. They may have left instructions about the type of service they would like. It is important to also take into account the sort of ceremony you or the rest of the family feel at peace with – a quiet gathering, or maybe an elaborate ceremony.

The funeral will be a time when the reality of what has happened can be too much to bear but it is also a time for saying goodbye to the person that has been taken from you. Remember, it is your choice whether the facts around your loved one's death are mentioned but, whatever you decide, the funeral will be an occasion for remembering their life and the love and affection you had for them.

Family Conflicts

Death brings out the best and worst in families. Conflict can begin even before your loved one dies, with disagreements about caregiving responsibilities. Everyone grieves in different ways, which can also be a major source of conflict within families. This is especially common if one family member thinks another is not as impacted by the death as they are, or that they are 'moving on' too quickly. Be aware that each family member had a different relationship with the person who died, and everyone grieves in their own way and at their own pace.

Decisions about the funeral are usually made by reference to a family hierarchy that starts with the deceased's spouse, who is then followed by children, parents, siblings and more distant relations. An executor named in the will can also decide about the funeral. The death of a loved one can often make people feel a loss of control, which can be terrifying, and some family members may seek to regain control by trying to plan the funeral without getting anyone else's input.

Decisions about whether someone will be buried or cremated, where the service will be held, the choice of music and poems, and even who will be invited can bring surprising upset between family members.

Communicating isn't always easy, but it is important in reducing conflict. Make a plan right away for how and when things will be handled. Agree on a time frame to all sit down together to go over the funeral arrangements and make a plan for regular updates and communication between you all.

Jack

When Jack died, his wife, ex-wife and their two sons all decided that their own individual wishes were more important than anyone else's when arranging his funeral. As the celebrant, I knew that his wife, Jean, was regarded as his next of kin and had the final say, but it was hard for everyone to keep their conflict out of the ceremony.

After a stressful family meeting, we decided that I would include as many of their wishes as possible in the thirty-minute ceremony time they had booked at the crematorium. It was agreed that both sons would share their memories of their dad at the wake after the funeral. They had chosen Jack's favourite pub, invited all his friends and had planned a slideshow of their lives together.

Jack's ex-wife had sent me a long speech of their life together, with hurtful references about Jean, but, thankfully, she decided not to stand up and share it on the day. They all agreed, though, that if Jack's brother became violent, the funeral director would step in to defuse the situation.

It was important to keep all of the family up to date with the ceremony so that, on the day, they all knew what to expect. Jack's funeral went ahead and – even though family members stood in their own groups after the ceremony and didn't communicate – they all separately thanked me for sharing their stories and what Jack had meant to them.

Top Tip

To ensure there is no conflict at your own ceremony, create your own funeral wishes and share them with your family (see Section 5.2 Funeral Wishes).

PART 5

Planning
and Wishes

5.1

———

End-of-Life Planning

*Remembering that I'll be dead soon is the most important tool
I've ever encountered to help me make big choices in life.*

—**Steve Jobs, Commencement Address**

It is never too early to make plans for your own end-of-life care and wishes. You never know what will happen in the future, so it is better to be prepared or any decisions may be taken out of your control.

Make Your Will

If you die without a will, the law decides who gets your assets, such as your house, possessions and money. You can write your will yourself, which can include who you want to benefit, who will look after any children under eighteen and the names of your executors who are going to carry out your wishes after your death.

If you want to include a charity in your will, Free Wills

Month (www.freewillsmonth.org.uk) brings together a number of charities to offer anyone aged fifty-five and over the opportunity to have simple wills written or updated free of charge. They do this by using participating solicitors in selected locations across England, Northern Ireland and Wales. You can also download a free will guide on the website, which leads you through the decision process or making a will in easy steps.

If your circumstances are not straightforward, you should get advice from a solicitor or employ a will writer. Make sure they are members of either The Society of Will Writers (www.willwriters.com), the Institute of Professional Will Writers (www.ipw.org.uk) or the Society of Trust and Estate Practitioners (www.step.org).

You also need to get your will formally witnessed and signed to make it legally valid. A copy of your will may be held with your solicitor or your bank, but make sure your next of kin also has a copy.

There is also a national will register known as Certainty (www.nationalwillregister.co.uk), which is a growing store for wills. It is used by the public, thousands of solicitors, charities and financial institutions to register and search for wills, ensuring your beneficiaries will then be able to access your will after your death. At the moment, Certainty have eight million wills registered.

Lasting Power of Attorney

A lasting power of attorney for property and financial affairs allows your loved ones to deal with paying your bills, buying and selling your property and managing your bank accounts and investments.

A lasting power of attorney for health and welfare covers decisions about health and care and even deciding where you are to live. This can only be used if you become incapable of dealing with such matters yourself.

You can complete and register the forms on the Office of the Public Guardian website (www.gov.uk/government/organisations/office-of-the-public-guardian), or speak to your own solicitor for more advice.

Folder of Documents

Tying up loose ends is to be encouraged as part of your funeral wishes. Create a folder to include your birth certificate, passport, driving licence, bank account details and recent bank statements (list all your accounts and account details), pension plans, insurance policies and your National Insurance number. Once you have made your will and lasting power of attorney, add these documents to the folder. Hand the folder to your next of kin or let them know where it is kept.

Top Tip

Put all your own contacts in an address book, and if your contacts are on your computer, make sure you leave the password in your folder.

Pre-Paid Funeral Plan

If you have signed up to a funeral plan with a local funeral director, keep all the details on file. Many people put aside the cost in a savings account instead and leave details with their next of kin.

Digital Legacy

Over the last few years, the internet has changed the way in which we communicate with each other. A digital legacy is the digital information that is available about someone following their death and can also be created or co-created by others. These may include:

- Website or blog listings
- Social media profiles
- Photos, videos, gaming profiles
- Online chats
- Friends' Facebook pages
- eBooks
- Cloud services

To find out more, The Digital Legacy Association (www.digitallegacyassociation.org) have created a number of tutorials that address the most popular digital devices and online services. They have a document for you to download to complete with all your online accounts, usernames and management, e.g. you may want some social media accounts to be deactivated, or close friends or family to be able to recover photographs stored online.

They also offer guides for each device and social media platform.

If you have an online bank account, your executors can arrange for it to be closed down and claim the money on behalf of your estate.

The charity Dying Matters (www.dyingmatters.org) has useful information and links about making a social media will. It is recommended, however, to include digital assets that have financial value within your will.

Sharing your digital legacy details with your next of kin will make their job so much easier. Making a note of your passwords to your music and photo collections will mean a lot to your friends and family as they may be able to use your ideas to personalise your funeral ceremony.

Organ Donation

If you would like to donate your organs, the best thing you can do is discuss your decision with your family. Organ donation is now automatic as the law requires all adults to become organ donors when they die but your decision can be registered on the NHS website (www.organdonation. nhs.uk/register-your-decision).

You can choose which organs to donate, including your lungs, kidneys, heart, liver, pancreas and/or small bowel. You can also donate tissues and even corneas. The cornea, the clear tissue at the front of each eye, is one type of tissue that is usually suitable for everyone to donate and could save and restore someone's eyesight.

You can also donate your brain, as scientists use brain tissue donated after death to better understand the causes of and treatment options for Alzheimer's disease and related dementias. Brains for Dementia Research (www.bdr.alzheimersresearchuk.org/brain-donors) has more information and local contact details for you to report the death to the Brain Bank.

By donating your organs and tissue after you die, you can save or improve as many as seventy-five lives. Anyone can donate organs; your age, health, faith or belief needn't stop you from registering your decision. Due to a shortage, it is especially important to consider becoming an organ donor if you belong to an ethnic minority.

Donating your Body to Medical Science

Body donations to medical schools can be used for teaching students or healthcare professionals about the structure and function of the human body. It can also be used for scientific research and training for surgical techniques. The government website has more details to help you make up your mind (www.hta.gov.uk).

If this is something you would like to do, contact a medical school in your local area, a tissue bank or research centre and ask them to provide you with the relevant paperwork to register your wish to donate your body. A complete copy of this paperwork should be kept with your will and funeral wishes document.

At the end of the research, medical schools will usually arrange for donated bodies to be cremated. Your family can also request the return of your body for a private burial or cremation. Medical schools may also hold a committal, memorial or thanksgiving service once a year.

Under some circumstances – for example, if you have certain health conditions or have recently undergone surgery – a medical school may not be able to accept your body, so make sure you have stated alternative arrangements for your funeral.

Advance Planning

There are several things you can do to ensure that your family know what you would like to happen near the end of your life. You can even decide what you do not want and who will speak for you. Talking about and recording your wishes in advance will mean that you still have control over your treatment even when you may be unable to make decisions yourself through illness or accident.

It is free to make an advance statement and advance decision, and there are many charities that will help you plan your end-of-life care, including the Alzheimer's Society (www.alzheimers.org.uk) who has a draft form you might like to use. Compassion in Dying (www.compassionindying.org.uk) can also provide forms or you can complete them online. The charity Advance Decisions Assistance (www.adassistance.org.uk) has been set up to raise awareness of advance decisions and to help people complete them.

Advance Decision to Refuse Treatment (Living Will)
As long as you are over eighteen years old, an advance decision (advance directive in Scotland) gives you the

legal right to refuse specific medical treatment in future in case you later become unable to make or communicate decisions for yourself, such as through a heart attack, stroke, road traffic accident or sporting injury.

They are particularly useful for anyone with a degenerative condition such as dementia or motor neurone disease who wants to plan ahead. Advance decisions have also been upheld by judges in court. In one case they ruled that a man with motor neurone disease who had lost the ability to communicate must have his ventilator removed, as his advance decision had specified.

You can also refuse treatment that replaces or supports ailing bodily functions, such as ventilation if you cannot breathe by yourself, CPR (cardiopulmonary resuscitation – a treatment used to try to restart a person's heart and/ or breathing) if your heart stops, and antibiotics that help your body fight infection.

Deciding to refuse a treatment is not the same as asking someone to end your life or help you end your life. Euthanasia and assisted suicide are illegal in the UK.

Top Tip

You may want to discuss your advance decision with a doctor or nurse who knows about your medical history before you make up your mind.

If you are refusing life-sustaining treatment, your advance decision must be in writing and include the words: 'my refusal applies even if my life is at risk or shortened as a result'. You must then sign and date your form in the presence of a witness, who must also sign and date the form.

Your witness can be anyone over the age of eighteen. Make sure your witness is not someone who will inherit your money or property after your death, such as a close relative or partner. To avoid someone later questioning if you were put under pressure to make your advance decision, your attorney (the person appointed to make decisions on your behalf through a lasting power of attorney) should also not be a witness.

The witness is not confirming that you have capacity to make the decisions in the form, they are just watching you sign your advance decision.

You can change your advance decision form at any time as your circumstances change. If you also have a lasting power of attorney set up, make sure they work together and one doesn't invalidate the other. The most recently signed and dated document will take precedence.

DNAR: Do Not Attempt Resuscitation
This form is not legally binding (unlike the advance decision) but informs healthcare professionals that they should not attempt CPR. They will still give you all other types of treatment for your condition so that you are comfortable and pain-free.

Advance Statement
An advance statement is a written statement that sets out your preferences, wishes, beliefs and values regarding

your future care. It will only be used if you are unable to tell people how you wish to be cared for. It can be updated at any time and can be made as a voice recording or even a video.

You can state whether you want to be cared for in a residential home, hospital or in your own home, and decide the care of your body after death.

It may include your hobbies and pastimes, spiritual beliefs, dietary needs, any goals you would like to complete before your death – in fact, anything that is important to your health and quality of life.

You can even write down things that you would prefer not to happen to you, such as any life-lengthening procedures when there is no need, or even something simple like the fact that you hate your hair to be stroked.

You may decide to have quiet music playing or your family sitting around your bed. If you have beliefs, rituals and customs around dying that are important to you, make sure you write them down, e.g. you may want your spiritual leader to be there, specific ceremonies to be performed, sacred songs to be sung or drums to be played. You can also decide to be on your own in silence – whatever is right for you.

Janie

Janie completed her advance statement and shared it with her family. She was very specific that, if possible, she wanted to die at home in her own bed:

- *Fresh flowers in the room, changed regularly.*
- *Candles lit in the evenings.*

- *Massage my hands and feet using scented cream, but don't stroke my hair!*
- *Natural light, lots of fresh air and a loose cotton nightdress.*
- *Food and drink to be shared, along with memories and funny stories of my life and what I have meant to them all.*
- *Champagne to be popped as I die and a toast to my journey into the next life.*
- *My ultimate dream is to die as they raise their glasses!*

Once Janie had made her statement, she told me that she felt relieved that her family knew what she wanted, and it also brought her closer to them all as they discussed her wishes together.

Your advance statement is not legally binding but your wishes will be taken into account and will only be used if you are unable tell your loved ones how and where you want to be cared for.

End-of-Life Doulas

You may request an end-of-life doula (www.eol-doula. uk) to be present to support you and your family so that your last days are as compassionate, calm, natural and as normal as they can be.

End-of-life doulas work in your home but also in hospices, hospitals and care homes. They do not replace medical support but add that missing layer, acting as a companion, an advocate, a mentor and a source of information and guidance. They can also help you write your advanced decisions and statement and have an emergency telephone line if you need help.

Pets

If you have pets, you may want to make arrangements for them to be cared for. The Dogs Trust suggests you choose someone to be your dog guardian, so that if you pass away or become seriously ill they can sign over ownership of your dog on your behalf. You then receive a free Canine Care Card to fill in with all the details.

Top Tip

The Cinnamon Trust also provides long-term care for pets if you have moved to residential accommodation that will not accept them.

Pet End-of-Life Support Before Death (PELS)

There are also end-of-life doulas for your pets (www.pels.info). If you know that your pet is in the last stages of their life and you require support through this difficult time, the doula will come to your home, create an end-of-life plan and spend time with you and your pet. They will advise you of what to expect, as well as giving you emotional and practical support. If you choose, the doula will also create and perform a beautiful ceremony before transporting your pet on your behalf to the crematorium or supporting you with burying them in your garden.

Sharing Your Decisions

Discuss all your decisions with the people closest to you as it helps make sure that they understand what you want and can respect your wishes. If you feel worried about discussing your end-of-life plans, let them know a few weeks beforehand that you would like the conversation so that they get used to the idea.

Start with day-to-day things such as the food you would like to eat or the clothes you would like to wear. Move the conversation on to what is important to you in your last days and hours of life and how you would like to be cared for.

As this is a sensitive subject, talk about your wishes in a series of shorter conversations. Take your time and come back to it another day if your loved ones are finding it hard. You may find that your family and friends are more in tune than you thought.

When Jenny was diagnosed with terminal cancer, she chose a long dog walk to discuss her end-of-life care with her husband, Leo. He felt able to respond as there was no pressure to fill any silences. By the end of the walk, they were laughing about inviting Jenny's belly-dancing group to the hospice in her last hours to lift everyone's spirits!

If you do not have anyone to talk to about your wishes, make sure they are written down and shared with your doctor and healthcare team. You can also contact Ageing Without Children (www.awwoc.org) as they provide support for people who have no families so that they have the resources they need. They also bring together people online through their Facebook group and local groups that meet on a monthly basis with speakers and social events.

It is good to share your decisions. Let your family and friends know that they will only have to act on your decisions if you lack the capacity to make them for yourself.

Top Tip

If you feel you cannot talk about your own wishes, highlight your choices in this book or fill in the My Plan section (see Part 6) with your decisions and hand it to your family and friends. They will then know what you would like to happen when you die.

Location of Documents

Give photocopies of your documents, as well as your registered lasting power of attorney form, to anyone who is regularly involved in your care and to people you know and trust.

Ask your GP to keep photocopies of your advanced decision and advanced statement with your medical records and to inform the relevant ambulance trust. Keep a copy with you; preferably the original so that you can review it regularly.

Compassion in Dying also offer a Notice of Advance Decision card to keep in your bag or wallet.

MedicAlert (www.medicalert.org.uk) provides jewellery for people who need to convey important medical information in an emergency.

Order a free 'Message in a Bottle' from Lions Club International (www.lionsclubs.co/Public/messsage-in-a-bottle) in which to keep a note of where your advance statement or advance decision documents are kept in the house. Keep the Bottle in your fridge – paramedics should know to look for it there when entering someone's house.

Contact your local ambulance service to find out if they can record your advance decision on their system. If you're treated by a paramedic in an emergency and are not able to communicate your treatment wishes to them, your advance decision on their system will make it more likely to be followed.

Top Tip

Find your local ambulance trust by contacting Compassion in Dying or view a list of all NHS authorities and trusts on the NHS website (www. nhs.uk).

Death Cafes

If you are unsure about talking about your own death then maybe you can go along to a Death Cafe (www. deathcafe.com) – a place where people gather to eat cake, drink tea and discuss death in a warm and relaxed setting. They are friendly gatherings where you can have conversations about hopes, fears and preferences about how you would want your death to be. Death Cafes are run on a voluntary basis. There is no agenda, just a place to go to talk about death, with cake. Since 2020, they are also meeting online.

Coffin Clubs

Coffin Clubs (www.coffinclub.co.uk) are also held around the UK. Their aim is to empower people to take control of their final send-off. They also have online resources, talks and courses to educate and inform everyone about all the options and choices that are available to them, as well as offering advice.

5.2

Funeral
Wishes

I want fireworks at my funeral
To brighten up your eyes
I want clowns at my funeral
To return all your smiles...

...So, party, party, party
And cheer my spirit with song
As my last wish is you celebrate
That life goes on

—Michael Ashby, 'Life Goes On'

We have so many different names for death and dying,
such as 'passing away', 'snuffing it', 'meeting your maker',
'kicking the bucket', 'croaking', 'giving up the ghost' and
'pushing up daisies', but when someone actually dies, no
one seems to know what to say.

It has been taboo in the past to mention death and
dying and, of course, we are all different. Many people do

128

not wish to be reminded of their inevitable death so never make a funeral plan. As an experienced funeral celebrant, I have met many families who had wished their loved one had made a plan as it makes their decisions much easier.

Gloria

I visited one family who told me that they had never talked about death in their family and their mum, Gloria, just asked to be 'put on the compost heap'. We created a beautiful ceremony based on their memories and classical music they thought their mum would have liked and everyone was happy.

However, two weeks later I had a phone call from one of the daughters to say that, in clearing their mum's house, they found her wishes in a bedside drawer and it bore no resemblance to their ceremony! She had wanted her brother to stand up and tell funny stories about their life together, 'Mr Sandman' sung by The Chordettes played in memory of meeting her husband and she wanted to go out to 'Hey Big Spender' by Shirley Bassey, as she loved spending money!

One of the most positive things you can do for yourself and your loved ones is to write your own funeral wishes, and you can use the My Plan section (see Part 6) of this book to do so. You can do this at any age and update the document over the years.

To give you ideas about your own funeral, draw on all the information in this book and look back at Part 2: Funeral Planning, Part 3: The Funeral Ceremony and Part 4: Specialised Ceremonies.

Funeral Planning

Make it clear whether you want to use a funeral director or would like your family or friends to look after all the arrangements.

Write down whether you want a natural burial, burial or cremation (see Section 2.2 Burial or Cremation) and state the addresses and contact details of your preferred burial sites or crematoria. Record your preference of type of coffin, shroud and any special decoration (see Section 2.3 The Coffin and Transport).

Write down how you want to be dressed (a favourite outfit, football shirt, scarf, etc.) and decide whether you want your body to be viewed or not.

Finally choose your method of transport to the funeral, e.g. motorcycle and sidecar, hearse, horse-drawn vehicle, or even your own Land Rover.

Decide where you wish your ashes to be scattered or interred and how and where you would like your family and friends to celebrate your life afterwards, e.g. afternoon tea at your local hotel.

Funeral Ceremony

Make a list of people you would like to invite. Are you planning a private ceremony or one that is open to everyone who ever knew you? If relevant, also make a list of people you do not want to be there.

State the type of funeral you would like, e.g. religious, spiritual, humanist or a combination of all three. If you have beliefs, rituals and customs that are important to you, make sure you have noted them down. Decide the type of celebrant you would like to officiate at the ceremony – religious, independent or humanist – and include the name of the celebrant if possible (see Section 3.1 Funeral Celebrants).

Write down your choices of music and why they are important to you. Maybe they remind you of people, places or special events or may even have helped you through difficult times.

Choose poems and readings and state the reason behind each one. Decide who you would like to read the poems and the eulogy. If you have left a personal message to everyone, decide who you would like to read it. You may want to choose a webcast or ask your loved ones to wear a favourite colour.

Decide any personal touches you would like, e.g. candles lit, flowers laid or doves released. Make a note of whether the curtains remain open or are closed at the end of the ceremony. (Read Section 3.2 Creating the Ceremony to help you with the planning.)

Top Tip

Donations are a personal choice, so state your preferred charity.

Life Stories
Memories fade, no matter how hard you hold onto them, so if it is important to you, write your own story to include

where you were born, your journey through life, what is important to you and what messages you would like to leave to your family and friends. Include stories each step of the way so that your memories are shared. You can even leave an audio or video recording to share with your loved ones.

Top Tip

Highlight a few photos that really reflect how you see yourself and ask that they be used in the order of service.

Write a list of all the important people in your life and what they mean to you. They can include family, friends, neighbours, teachers, colleagues and pets. Some of these people will still be with you and others may be out of touch. Include memories of each person and how they impacted on your journey through life. Sometimes the stories would be lost if they are not shared for a future generation.

Include lessons learnt, challenges faced, who helped you along the way, who inspired you. Add your proudest moments, trophies, qualifications, new babies, moments featured in the news, shared in the family or even gone unnoticed to everyone but yourself. As long as they mattered to you, include them.

Describe your character in a few words – loving, kind, stubborn, single-minded – and which character trait you are most proud of. Write down your talents and skills and how you have used them throughout life, your values, the issues you care about and your spiritual beliefs.

The following stories are from real ceremonies to encourage you to share your own memories.

Delsie

As the war created food shortages, Delsie and her family foraged for food in the fields and on Wembury beach. Her mum would send her to the shop to buy their cheese rations and, by the time she had got home again, most of the cheese had been eaten. After that incident, her mother used to keep the butter and cheese in her apron pocket to stop the children eating them!

Dennis

Dennis was an electrician on the docks and he used to tell the story that one day he was fixing a big capstan and had an accident that cut off his leg. He saved his own life by tying his belt around the wound and stopping the bleeding with his silver cigarette case. He was awarded a medal for saving his own life.

Betty and Bill

Betty and Bill bought a tandem and cycled from Croydon to Brighton and back. No one believed they had cycled so far, so they repeated the journey, making sure they brought back a stick of rock from Brighton as proof.

Joan

Paul and his brother shared the story of the time their mother, Joan, once cycled after them to the station with their forgotten packed lunches. The crossing gates were closed and, with no footbridge to the opposite platform where the boys were waiting, Joan threw the lunch packets over the tracks to land at their feet. Paul and Eric were so embarrassed to see their mother was still wearing her nightie and dressing gown!

Bucket List

Create a bucket list of things you have not achieved already and would like to do before you die, such as riding in a hot-air balloon, swimming with dolphins or travelling to Japan. If you don't manage to complete your list, decide which of your friends and loved ones you would like to carry on your adventures.

Legacies

You may have already inherited legacies from people now dead or no longer known to you. They could be material things like books, ornaments or money. They may be mementoes like letters or postcards, but they are more likely to be stories handed down through the family about events, people or days out.

As important is the legacy that you leave to other people: your children, grandchildren, friends and relatives. Maybe you have taught your grandchildren how to swim, create a picture or bake a cake. You may have handed on your love of music, books or nature. Your family could have learnt that you are a strong, brave person with a great sense of humour and realised that they would like to be more like you.

Legacies can also include: leaving money to build a library, buying a village a goat or a well, planting a tree, naming a star, adopting an animal, setting up a scholarship or trophy, recording a song or leaving money to charity.

Family Tree

You can even include your own family tree, possibly tracing your ancestors back to Norman the Conqueror! There are many organisations, websites and books that will help you and they all suggest you start by talking to your own family first. If you have created your own family tree, the next generations will benefit.

Ancestry DNA Test

Consider taking an ancestry DNA test to give your family an insight into their past. The results include information about your geographic origins and identifies potential relatives through DNA matching to others if they have taken the test. Your results could be a great starting point for further family history research.

Memory Book

Another way of leaving a legacy is to create your own memory book to include photos, stories, memories or even tickets and programmes from theatre trips and holidays. Not only do you get to enjoy your memories while you are still alive, you can leave it for others to enjoy when you are gone.

Memory Box

Create your own memory box of items you treasure and the stories behind them. Include suggestions of what you would like to happen to them after you die. Maybe your football scarf is to be passed on to your grandson who always accompanies you to the matches? Your gold pendant to your best friend who has always admired it? One ninety-five-year-old lady stuck labels on all her belongings with names of her family written on each one – at least everyone knew what she wanted!

Legacy Letters

As you plan your own funeral, think of the messages you would like to leave to your loved ones. You could create legacy letters, which may include your favourite recipe (maybe handed on from your grandma), the title of a book or film that meant so much to you, or even your best joke for your family to keep alive.

Your letter doesn't have to be a literary masterpiece. Write from the heart and include your favourite memory of being with each person and something you have learnt that you would like them to know. As the author Sharon L. Alder said: 'Carve your name on hearts, not tombstones. A legacy is etched into the minds of others and the stories they share about you.'

Start from the beginning of your life; tell stories about your parents and grandparents and your early days. What physical characteristics have you received from them to hand on to your family – blonde hair, big feet, work ethic, sense of humour?

As you have done in your life story, include the strengths

that make you special, such as determination, love of music or spirituality. Think about the characteristics, talents and values that you are passing on to your loved ones: a love of sport, optimism, sense of compassion or even a lack of eyebrows.

Tell your loved ones how much you've learnt from life and offer the gift of your learning, experience and values to them all. Include one thing you regret and one thing you are most proud of. Tell them how much they have meant to you and even give them a blessing. If there are any milestones that you may be absent for, what practical information or advice will help your loved ones in these situations?

Maybe you just want to die with a clean slate, with no grudges or hard feelings, so write a letter to each family member, sharing memories and wishes for their future, and arrange for the letters to be given to them before the funeral. These can be letters full of gratitude and even apologies to loved ones.

Pamela
After chatting with her friends about her funeral wishes for a couple of hours, Pamela decided to contact her daughter in Canada as a first step towards reconciliation.

Keep your handwritten letter safe, as well as providing digital and backup copies. That way, your family can share them among themselves and read them whenever they please.

Barry

Barry included letters to his grandchildren to be opened on future big occasions – first job, getting married, special birthdays – just to tell them how proud he was of them. He hoped to deliver the letters in person, but was glad to put it all into words first. He has given copies of the letters to his son, Andy, to hand out to all the family after his funeral.

Jenna

Jenna, a Brown Owl for many years, has devised a treasure hunt for her family to follow and find the letters in her house after her death, so that they can receive them all together.

Top Tip

Sharing your letter with a trusted friend for feedback is a good idea. Remember, you can always update legacy letters in the future.

Online Store

Consider using Keylu (www.keylu.com), an online store for all your important information, which makes it available to the right people at the right time after your death. You can store information about your bank accounts, utilities, savings, insurance – all of the things that you manage on a day-to-day basis. You can list personal items and who you would like them to be left to.

Share Your Wishes

When you have completed your funeral wishes document, sign and date it. Make sure that you hand your wishes to your next of kin, close friend or family member so that, when you die, they know exactly what you wanted and do not have to guess.

> **Margaret**
> *Margaret, who was in her fifties, wrote on her funeral wishes:*
>
> * *No fuss, music or poems*
> * *Eco-coffin for cremation*
> * *Family to have tea afterwards and, maybe, share memories*
> * *Will in filing cabinet*
> * *Donor card in purse.*
>
> *If I still have friends who wish to say goodbye to me, I wish to be cremated and have a small service. If I am old, ancient and a pain in the ——, a cremation will be enough, and then you all go out and celebrate!*

Only time will tell what will happen!

David Bowie shared his wishes before he died and he had exactly what he wanted: a private cremation and his ashes scattered in Bali, in line with Buddhist rituals. His family were happy to fulfil his wishes, which didn't stop his friends and many fans all over the world paying tribute in their own way to his life and legacy.

There are so many choices and ideas now that Joe, who is in his fifties, said he wished he could be there as it all sounded so exciting. Thankfully he can update the document over the years, just in case his choice of The Stranglers singing 'Nice and Sleazy' doesn't appeal when he is in his eighties!

It is worth remembering that, even though you may have written and planned every detail of your funeral, circumstances may get in the way. In 2020, Covid restricted the number of mourners at funeral ceremonies and get-togethers afterwards were unable to go ahead. A final thought is, if you are planning a slap-up meal for one hundred people, make sure you have money set aside to pay for it.

Of course, you may not want to wait until you have gone, so why not plan a party to celebrate your life and pay tribute to everyone who has played such a big part in it? (See Section 5.3 Living Ceremonies.)

5.3

Living
Ceremonies

I'd like the memory of me to be a happy one.
I'd like to leave an afterglow of smiles when life is done.

—Helen Lowrie Marshall

When someone is born, we celebrate their entrance into our world and our lives. We celebrate each year that passes with birthday parties, marking the annual ceremony of when someone's life began. Why should the end of life be any different? Why focus on the negative aspect of a person leaving us when we should look back and celebrate all that they have accomplished?

Every person has their own ideas about what constitutes a good life – and its end – and it is important to acknowledge the opinions of all members of the family. By talking about these ideas, everyone feels they are being heard and are contributing to the ceremony. Sometimes a group discussion is all it takes to share ideas, but be prepared to have private talks afterwards for family members who have less confidence.

The following stories are from real ceremonies to give you ideas and encourage you to create your own ceremony.

Margaret

I was asked to perform a ceremony for a terminally ill lady who lived on Dartmoor. I drove through leafy lanes and over the moors to find their beautiful house, where Margaret was sitting in her wheelchair surrounded by her family. I explained what they could expect at a living ceremony: they could acknowledge important relationships, recount stories, and give and receive comfort. Margaret could smell the flowers, hear the eulogy, readings and music, and see the photographs. She could also speak of her own life and legacy; about what mattered to her and motivated or inspired her over her lifetime, and about what her relationships have meant to her. For everyone there it would be a time to honour and appreciate the living Margaret before she died.

Her family rose to the challenge and organised a celebration fit for a queen. They had a marquee in the garden, a slideshow with family photographs dating from Margaret's childhood, all the food was prepared by family and friends, memories were shared by the guests – some who had prepared beforehand and some who just stood up and spoke. Her daughters had picked flowers from her garden and used them to decorate the many tables in the marquee. We raised our glasses of Prosecco to Margaret and cheered.

Everyone there agreed they were grateful for the opportunity not only to bid Margaret a fond farewell, but also to celebrate the life of a woman who was, in all ways, unique and very special. It honoured her deep intelligence, humour and originality, as well as the joy she had always brought to all aspects of life, and those fortunate enough to encounter her on her journey through life.

Within a month Margaret had died and we all met again at her funeral to celebrate her life. Her daughter told me that throughout the ceremony she realised the true value of the life about to end and how the approaching separation would affect their own lives.

Doreen

Doreen loved Christmas, and this year she knew she wouldn't be around to celebrate it with her family as she was now in a hospice. So, in June, her family and friends brought Christmas to Doreen in the hospice. It was a joy to see the Christmas tree full of twinkling lights with an angel at the top. Everyone arrived wearing Christmas jumpers and party clothes, clutching presents and percussion instruments. The staff were amazing and had arranged a special tea, complete with crackers. Everyone present sang along to a karaoke Christmas CD as Doreen's guests played jingle bells and drums. The next day, Doreen told her daughter that she was now ready to die as she had accomplished everything she wanted and shared her love with her entire family.

Hannah

Hannah wanted to celebrate her life with a large gathering of family and friends at her favourite beach.

Her family hosted a picnic, with everyone bringing one of Hannah's favourite dishes to share. They organised a rounders game as other guests went swimming, then, in the evening, they all gathered together to share stories of Hannah as the sun set over the water.

Hannah sat in her wheelchair by a large basket full of her favourite pottery, ornaments, books and paintings. During the afternoon, family and friends came up to Hannah to share memories before choosing a memento to take home.

Her son, Aaron, took photos and a video of the day, which was included in her funeral a few months later. He also told everyone that he was going to have a tattoo party where each of Hannah's children would design a tattoo that reminded them of their mother, then they would visit the tattoo parlour together as a final tribute to their mum.

Having a living ceremony doesn't mean there can't be a traditional funeral after death. It simply means that there is a ceremony with the person before they are gone. They get to enjoy life with those they love before they must go, and hopefully pass with renewed good memories and the feeling that they've made peace with their life, peace with those in their life, and peace with their eventual death.

PART 6

My Plan

Use the following pages to write down your wishes for your own end-of-life ceremony, and any instructions that you would like your family and friends to follow after your death. Turn back through the pages of this book for inspiration.

PART 7

Conclusion

7.1

Conclusion

We will look for you in the stars…
Perhaps they are not stars in the sky,
but rather openings where our loved ones shine down
to let us know that they are happy.

—Eskimo Proverb

When someone we love dies, we may rebel against it at first as we may not want to accept that the person we loved is gone. At a personal and meaningful funeral, mourners have the chance to confront reality and begin to process their grief. The funeral is not the end of the grief journey, though; it is just the beginning.

Almost all cultures and all countries have ceremonies to mark the more important stages of our lives. They celebrate life's essential moments, reflect on our beliefs, hopes, traditions, culture and spirituality, and express who we are. It's part of the human experience to mark times of positive and negative change.

Rituals play a significant part in our lives, and such celebrations help to generate a bond between all those who participate: they enable us to define new roles and help us to acknowledge new relationships and responsibilities. When a spouse dies, their partner becomes someone who is single. A funeral allows everyone to support the mourner in their new status. It also strengthens the community network and allow us to get to know each other better. Even trauma bonds people during these occasions because it reinforces social ties and empathy.

The funeral ceremony shows people that they are united and that they belong. It also makes us think about our own lives and how we want to spend our remaining days. Ceremonies are about expressing gratitude for the people we love and being thankful for the opportunity of spending time with them. That sense of gratitude can make the experience much richer.

Having a funeral ceremony is key to remembering our loved one through the eulogy, in the music or poems chosen. We gather with other people who knew our loved one, we can share our memories, give voice to our feelings, and find support in others. A funeral ceremony acts as a safe place for us to get our thoughts and emotions out.

Throughout this book I have shown how you can plan your own funeral as well as celebrate a loved one's life, before and after they have gone. Every person has a different idea of what is important to them and it is essential to include their beliefs and wishes in each ceremony so that it becomes a personalised, meaningful and healing way to say goodbye.

Death is an unavoidable part of the cycle of life, but by coming to terms with the inevitability of death it can help teach us to live more fully in the here and now and enable us to cherish every moment of the life we have.

PART 8

Helpful
Resources

8.1

Counselling and Support

Barnardo's Child Bereavement Service
Advice to help deal with loss of a child or young person up to the age of eighteen
23 Windsor Avenue, Belfast BT9 6EE
Tel: 028 9066 8333
Email: catherine.meighan@barnardos.org.uk
Website: www.barnardos.org.uk

Bereavement Advice Centre
Practical advice for what to do after a death
Bereavement Advice Centre, Heron House, Timothy's Bridge Road, Stratford Upon Avon CV37 9BX
Tel: 0800 634 9494
Website: www.bereavementadvice.org

Bereavement Trust
A helpline with trained volunteers offering comfort, support and practical advice to the bereaved
Tel: 0800 435455

British Association for Counselling and Psychotherapy

Helping people make better, more informed choices about the provision of counselling and raising the ethical and professional standards of the profession

15 St John's Business Park, Lutterworth, Leicestershire LE17 4HB

Tel: 01455 883300

Email: bacp@bacp.co.uk

Website: www.bacp.co.uk

Cherished Gowns UK

Creating beautiful items of clothing for babies that have passed away

7 Park Pl, Dover CT16 1DF

Tel: 01304 201154

Website: www.cherishedgowns.org.uk

Child Bereavement UK

Helping children and young people (up to age twenty-five), parents and families, to rebuild their lives when a child grieves, or when a child dies

Child Bereavement UK, Unit B Knaves Beech Way, Knaves Beech Industrial Estate, Loudwater, High Wycombe, Bucks HP10 9QY

Tel: 0800 02 888 40

Email: enquiries@childbereavementuk.org

Website: www.childbereavementuk.org

The Child Death Helpline
A freephone service for all those affected by the death of a child
Barclay House, 37 Queen Square, London WC1N 3BH
Tel: 0800 282 986
Email: contact@childdeathhelpline.org
Website: www.childdeathhelpline.org.uk

Childhood Bereavement Network
The hub for those working with bereaved children, young people and their families across the UK
National Children's Bureau, 23 Mentmore Terrace, London E8 3PN
Email: cbn@ncb.org.uk
Website: www.childhoodbereavementnetwork.org.uk

The Compassionate Friends
Support following the death of a child
14 New King Street, Deptford, London SE8 3HS
Tel: 0345 123 2304
Email: info@tcf.org.uk
Website: www.tcf.org.uk

Counselling Directory
Connecting you with help for your mental health
Counselling Directory Building 3, Riverside Way, Camberley, Surrey GU15 3YL
Tel: 0333 325 2500
Website: www.counselling-directory.org.uk

Cruse Bereavement Care

Support, advice and information for children, young people and adults when someone dies

Tel: 0808 808 1677

Website: www.cruse.org.uk

Daddy's with Angels

Providing support and guidance to all family members affected by the loss of a child at any age, but especially for bereaved dads

The Angel Office, The Gary Kay Centre, Spinning Gate, Leigh WN7 4PG

Tel: 07832517213

Website: www.daddyswithangels.org

Depression Alliance

Providing comprehensive resources to help people overcome depression

212 Spitfire Studios, 63–71 Collier Street, London N1 9BE

Tel: 0845 123 23 20

Email: information@depressionalliancce.org

Website: www.depressionalliance.org

The Good Grief Trust

Helps all those affected by grief in the UK. They have brought all bereavement services together around the country to ensure that everyone receives the support they need

Tel: 0800 2600 400

Email: hello@thegoodgrieftrust.org

Website: www.thegoodgrieftrust.org

Grief Encounter
Free support available to everyone and anyone suffering a bereavement
Crystal House, Daws Lane, London NW7 4ST
Tel: 0808 802 0111
Email: grieftalk@griefencounter.org.uk
Website: www.griefencounter.org.uk

Hope Again
Information and resources for young people who have been bereaved
Tel: 0808 808 1677
Email: helpline@cruse.org.uk
Website: www.hopeagain.org.uk

The Lions Barber Collective
An international group of barbers who have undergone training in how to recognise symptoms of mental ill health in clients and signpost them to relevant support services
Lions HQ, 11 Vaughan's Parade, Torquay Harbourside, Devon, TQ2 5EG
Email: info@thelionsbarbercollective.com
Website: www.thelionsbarbercollective.com

The Lullaby Trust
Raises awareness of sudden infant death syndrome (SIDS), provides expert advice on safer sleep for babies and offers emotional support for bereaved families
11 Belgrave Road, London SW1V 1RB
Tel: 0808 802 6868

Email: support@lullabytrust.org.uk
Website: www.lullabytrust.org.uk

The Mental Health Foundation
Helps people to understand, protect and sustain their mental health
Colechurch House, 1 London Bridge Walk, London SE1 2SX
Tel: 020 7803 1100
Website: www.mentalhealth.org.uk

Mind
Provides advice and support to empower anyone experiencing a mental health problem. Campaigns to improve services, raise awareness and promote understanding
15–19 Broadway, Stratford, London E15 4BQ
Tel: 0300 123 3393
Email: info@mind.org.uk
Website: www.mind.org.uk

The Miscarriage Association
Provides support following a miscarriage
17 Wentworth Terrace, Wakefield, WF1 3QW
Tel: 01924 200 799
Email: info@miscarriageassociation.org.uk
Website: www.miscarriageassociation.org.uk

National Bereavement Partnership
Provides a support helpline, counselling referral and befriending service for all those suffering from bereavement, grief, living loss, mental health issues, and

those affected by the COVID-19 pandemic
Tel: 0800 448 0800
Website: www.nationalbereavementpartnership.org

NHS Bereavement Helpline
Offers support and advice to families, friends and carers from trained nurses
Tel: 0800 2600 400

Rethink Mental Illness
Aims to improve the lives of people severely affected by mental illness through a network of local groups and services, expert information and successful campaigning
89 Albert Embankment, London SE1 7TP
Tel: 0808 801 0525
Website: www.rethink.org

The Rosie Crane Trust
Provides support for bereaved parents. Offers a twenty-four-hour 'Listening Ear Helpline', available to all in the UK. Drop-in centres are available in Somerset, North Dorset and North Devon in England
Rosie Crane Trust, PO Box 62, Ilminster, Somerset, TA19 0WW
Tel: 01460 55120
Email: contact@rosiecranetrust.co.uk
Website: www.rosiecranetrust.org

Samaritans
Help and support for anyone at any time
Freepost SAMARITANS LETTERS

Tel: 116 123
Email: jo@samaritans.org
Website: www.samaritans.org

The Stillbirth and Neonatal Death Society (SANDS)
Provides support for those affected by the death of a baby
Victoria Charity Centre, 11 Belgrave Road, London
SW1V 1RB
Tel: 0808 164 3332
Email: helpline@sands.org.uk
Website: www.sands.org.uk

Survivors of Bereavement by Suicide
Aims to meet the needs and overcome the isolation experienced by people over eighteen who have been bereaved by suicide
The Flamsteed Centre, Albert Street, Ilkeston, Derbyshire
DE7 5GU
Tel: 0300 111 5065
Email: email.support@uksobs.org
Website: www.uksobs.org

Suicide Bereavement UK
Carries out suicide bereavement research, provides consultancy on postvention (care of those bereaved by suicide) and develops and delivers evidence-based suicide bereavement training
6–8 Taper Street, Ramsbottom, Lancashire BL0 9EX
Tel: 01706 827 359
Website: www.suicidebereavementuk.com

Switchboard LGBT
Support following the death of a same-sex partner
PO Box 7324, London N1 9QS
Tel: 0300 330 0630
Email: admin@switchboard.lgbt
Website: www.switchboard.lgbt

Victim Support
An independent charity dedicated to supporting victims of crime and traumatic incidents in England and Wales
Tel: 08081689111
Website: www.victimsupport.org.uk

WAY Widowed And Young
A UK charity that offers a peer-to-peer support network for anyone who's lost a partner before their fifty-first birthday
Suite 14, College Business Centre, Uttoxeter New Road, Derby DE22 3WZ
Website: www.widowedandyoung.org.uk

Winston's Wish
Support for children and young people after the death of a parent or sibling
Tel: 08088 020 021
Email: ask@winstonswish.org
Website: www.winstonswish.org

8.2

Funeral
Advice

The Good Funeral Guide
*The UK's only not-for-profit independent information
resource for funeral advice*
Website: www.goodfuneralguide.co.uk

Help with Funeral Costs

Child Funeral Charity
*Help with costs of a funeral for a baby or child aged
sixteen or under*
Unit 1, The Shield Office Centre, 186a Station Road,
Burton Latimer, Kettering NN15 5NT
Tel: 01480 276088
Email: enquiries@childfuneralcharity.org.uk
Website: www.childfuneralcharity.org.uk

Children's Funeral Fund

Help with some of the costs of a funeral for a child under eighteen or a baby stillborn after the twenty-fourth week of pregnancy
Website: www.gov.uk/child-funeral-costs

Funeral Expenses Payment

You could get a Funeral Expenses Payment (also called a Funeral Payment) if you get certain benefits and need help to pay for a funeral you're arranging
Website: www.gov.uk/funeral-payments

Natural Burial

The Natural Death Centre
Independent Funeral Advice

Help, support, advice or guidance on planning a funeral, either for yourself or for someone close to you
In The Hill House, Watley Lane, Twyford, Winchester, SO21 1QX
Tel: 01962 712690
Email: contact@naturaldeath.org.uk
Website: www.naturaldeath.org.uk

Promessa

An environmentally friendly and ethical improvement to both burial and cremation
Email: info@promessa.se
Website: www.promessa.se

Recomposting
Known as natural organic reduction or human composting
Tel: +1 (206) 800–TREE
Email: info@recompose.life
Website: www.recompose.life

Resomation
Known as natural water cremation, this is the sustainable end-of-life choice that gently returns the body to ashes through a natural process using water
Tel: 0113 205 7422
Email: info@resomation.com
Website: www.resomation.com

Burial at Sea

Marine Management Organisation
Gain government permission to be buried at sea in the UK marine area
Website: www.gov.uk/guidance/how-to-get-a-licence-for-a-burial-at-sea-in-england

Coffins

Bellacouche
A unique range of biodegradable coffin alternatives for natural burial or cremation
The Unitarian Chapel, Cross Street, Moretonhampstead, Devon TQ13 8NL

Tel: 07763 935 897
Email: info@bellacouche.com
Website: www.bellacouche.com

Creative Coffins
Environmentally friendly beautiful cardboard coffins, in a range of designs or personalised for your loved one
Tel: 01481 714820
Email: post@creativecoffins.com
Website: www.creativecoffins.co.uk

Ecoffins
Beautifully handcrafted, environmentally friendly coffins and caskets
Garland House, Rawling Street, Milstead, Sittingbourne, Kent ME9 0RT
Tel: 01795 830688
Email: info@ecoffins.co.uk
Website: www.ecoffins.co.uk

Greenfield Creations Ltd
Provides a range of coffins created from cardboard, wicker or wood
Chapel Road, Ridgewell, Essex CO9 4RU
Tel: 01440 788 866
Email: info@greenfieldcreations.co.uk
Website: www.greenfieldcreations.co.uk

Loop Biotech
Coffins made of mycelium, which are biodegradable, provide nutrients to the plants growing around it and

it can clean up soil by converting waste products into nutrients

Molengraaffsingel 12, 2629 JD Delft, The Netherlands

Tel: +31 6 21 36 16 71

Email: info@loop-biotech.com

Website: www.loop-of-life.com

Willow Coffins

Willow coffins made entirely by hand, using traditional techniques

Somerset Willow England, The Wireworks Estate, Bristol Road, Bridgwater Somerset, TA6 4AP

Tel: 01278 424003

Email: enquiries@somersetwillow.co.uk

Website: www.somersetwillowcoffins.co.uk

Scattering and Interring of Ashes

Aura Flights

A unique space burial service that launches ashes to the edge of space and releases them to travel the world on a breathtaking final journey

Tel: 0114 213 1050

Email: info@auraflights.com.

Website: www.ashesinspace.co.uk

Cherished Urns

Providing urns for adults, children and pets, including water-soluble and biodegradable urns

Penstraze Business Centre, Truro, Cornwall TR4 8PN

Tel: 01872 487101
Email: hello@cherished-urns.co.uk
Website: www.cherished-urns.co.uk

Eternal Reefs
A designed reef made of environmentally safe cast concrete placed on the ocean floor as a permanent memorial of a life well lived
P.O. Box 3811, Sarasota, FL 34230-3811
Tel: 1-888-423-7333
Website: www.eternalreefs.com

The Long Barrow at All Cannings
A large structure made of natural materials to store urns of cremated remains
Woodway Drove, Devizes SN10 3NP
Tel: 01380 860483
Email: tim.daw@gmail.com
Website: www.thelongbarrow.com

Scattering Ashes
Advice, ashes jewellery, garden memorials and urns for water, burial and the home
The Chapel, 11 Seale Hayne, Newton Abbot Devon TQ12 6NQ
Tel: 01626 798198
Email: info@scattering-ashes.co.uk
Website: www.scattering-ashes.co.uk

Urns for Ashes
Personal urns and memorials, including biodegradable urns
Kidlington, Oxford OX5 1DH
Tel: 01865 600207
Email: support@urnsforashes.co.uk
Website: www.urnsforashes.co.uk

Funeral Celebrants

Association of Independent Celebrants
Includes a directory of celebrants
PO Box 116, Barton Upon Humber, North Lincolnshire,
DN18 9AL
Tel: 07469 192 644
Email: admin@independentcelebrants.com
Website: www.independentcelebrants.com

Funeral Celebrancy Council
A central organisation, defining best practice, representing funeral celebrants across the UK and setting high standards
Website: www.funeralcelebrancycouncil.org.uk

Humanists UK
Bringing non-religious people together to develop their own views and an understanding of the world around them
39 Moreland Street, London EC1V 8BB
Tel: 020 7324 3060
Email: ceremonies@humanism.org.uk
Website: www.humanism.org.uk

Institute of Civil Funerals
Independent civil funeral celebrants
Lytchett House, 13 Freeland Park, Wareham Road, Poole, Dorset, BH16 6FA
Tel: 01480 861411
Email: admin@iocf.org.uk
Website: www.iocf.org.uk

Funeral Directors

NAFD – National Association of Funeral Directors
The NAFD supports its members in arranging meaningful funerals, and caring for bereaved people, providing advice, advocacy and support
618 Warwick Road, Solihull B91 1AA
Tel: 0121 711 1343
Email: info@nafd.org.uk
Website: www.nafd.org.uk

SAIF – The National Society of Allied and Independent Funeral Directors
Upholding the UK's highest standards among independent funeral directors
SAIF Business Centre, 3 Bullfields, Sawbridgeworth, Herts CM21 9DB
Tel: 0345 230 6777
Email: info@saif.org.uk
Website: www.saif.org.uk

Military Funerals

Help for Heroes
Helping wounded veterans and their families to recover and get on with their lives
Unit 14 Parkers Close, Downton Business Centre, Salisbury, Wiltshire SP5 3RB
Tel: 0300 030 9888
Website: www.helpforheroes.org.uk

Royal British Legion
Advice and help with military and veterans' funerals
Tel: 0808 802 8080
Website: www.britishlegion.org.uk

Home Funerals

The Home Funeral Network UK
Offers support, education and guidance for all those involved in arranging a home based, family-led funeral
Website: www.homefuneralnetwork.org.uk

Only With Love
Support and guidance in caring for your loved one at home and the funeral
Tel: 01865 362984 / 07881641583
Email: claire@onlywithlove.co.uk
Website: www.onlywithlove.co.uk

8.3

Care

for Pets

Cats Protection
The UK's leading cat welfare charity, rehoming thousands of cats each year
National Cat Centre, Lewes Road, Chelwood Gate, Haywards Heath RH17 7TT
Tel: 03000 12 12 12
Website: www.cats.org.uk

The Cinnamon Trust
The National Charity for the elderly, the terminally ill and their pets
Tel: 01736 757 900
Website: www.cinnamon.org.uk

Dogs Trust
Dog rehoming services
17 Wakley Street, London, EC1V 7RQ
Tel: 020 7837 0006
Email: info@dogstrust.org.uk

Website: www.dogstrust.org.uk

Pet End-of-Life Support before Death (PELS)
Support and guidance when your pet is near the end of their life and after death
Tel: 07981 265 352
Email: lyonhawk19@gmail.com
Website: www.pels.info

8.4

Valuable
Help

The Bereavement Register
Can reduce the amount of unwanted marketing post being sent to those that have passed, stopping painful daily reminders
FREEPOST RTEU-JSHJ-LCTZ, 1 Newhams Row, London SE1 3UZ
Tel: 020 7089 6403
Automated phone line registration service: 0800 082 1230
Email: help@thebereavementregister.org.uk
Website: www.thebereavementregister.org.uk

Citizens Advice
Offers advice on what to do after a death, dealing with the financial affairs of someone who has died, funeral services, wills and what to do if someone dies abroad
Tel: 0800 144 8848
Website: www.citizensadvice.org.uk

Digital Legacy
The professional body for digital assets planning and digital legacy safeguarding
Tel: 01525 630349
Website: www.digitallegacyassociation.org

Dying Matters
Resources for everyone who wants to help raise awareness and promote conversation about death, dying and bereavement
Tel: 08000 21 44 66
Website: www.dyingmatters.org

Much Loved
An online memorial and tribute charity
The MuchLoved Charitable Trust, Nash House, Repton Place, White Lion Road, Amersham, Buckinghamshire HP7 9LP
Tel: 01494 722818
Website: www.muchloved.com

Tell Us Once
A service that lets you report a death to most government organisations in one go
Website: www.gov.uk/after-a-death/organisations-you-need-to-contact-and-tell-us-once

8.5

End-of-Life
Planning

Advance Decisions Assistance
A charity working to raise awareness of advance decisions ('living wills') and to help people complete them
ADA c/o Professor Celia Kitzinger, Department of Law and Politics, Cardiff University, Law Building, Museum Ave, Cardiff CF10 3AX
Tel: 01768 775566
Email: info@ADassistance.org.uk
Website: www.adassistance.org.uk

Age UK
Provide advice and information for people in later life through the Age UK Advice line, publications and website
Tel: 0800 169 65 65
Website: www.ageuk.org.uk

Ageing Without Children
For people who have not had children through choice, fertility or circumstance; people who have had children that have predeceased them, live a great distance away or have care needs of their own; or those with children unwilling to offer help and support
Email: info@awoc.org.uk
Website: www.awwoc.org

Alzheimer's Society
Offers advice, information and support in England and Wales to people with dementia, their families and carers through its helpline and local offices
Alzheimer's Society, Scott Lodge, Scott Road, Plymouth, PL2 3DU
Tel: 0333 150 3456
Website: www.alzheimers.org.uk

Ancestry DNA Test
Take an ancestry DNA test to give your family an insight into their past
Website: www.ancestry.co.uk/dna

Brains for Dementia Research
An initiative funded jointly by Alzheimer's Society and Alzheimer's Research UK to support brain donation and provide much-needed brain tissue for researchers
Brains for Dementia Research Coordinating Centre Rm EG02, Edwardson Building, Institute of Neuroscience, Newcastle University, Campus for Ageing and Vitality, Newcastle upon Tyne, NE4 5PL

Tel: 0191 208 2109
Email: BDR.Coordinatingcentre@ncl.ac.uk
Website: www.bdr.alzheimersresearchuk.org

Coffin Club
Informs people of all the choices available to them around their end-of-life funeral celebration. They also sell flat-pack coffins to assemble at home
Website: www.coffinclub.co.uk

Compassion in Dying
Help you prepare for the end of life: how to talk about it, plan for it and record your wishes
181 Oxford Street, London W1D 2JT
Tel: 0800 999 2434
Email: info@compassionindying.org.uk
Website: www.compassionindying.org.uk

Death Cafes
To increase awareness of death with a view to helping people make the most of their lives
Website: www.deathcafe.com

End-of-Life Doula
Facilitating an end of life that is as peaceful, graceful, meaningful and dignified as it can be
Website: www.eol-doula.uk

Gov.uk Lasting Power of Attorney
Download the forms and guidance to make and register a lasting power of attorney

Tel: 0300 456 0300
Email: customerservices@publicguardian.gsi.gov.uk
Website: www.gov.uk/government/publications/make-a-lasting-power-of-attorney

Human Tissue Authority
Information about donating your body to a medical school after death
2 Redman Place, London E20 1JQ.
020 7269 1900 (Monday to Friday, 9am to 5pm).
Tel: 020 0769 1900
Website: www.hta.gov.uk

Keylu
Enables you to get your personal, legal and financial affairs in order, to ensure those closest to you have access, and to create and manage your legacy
Square Sail House, Saint Austell PL25 3NJ
Website: www.keylu.com

Law Society
The independent professional body for solicitors
The Law Society's Hall, 113 Chancery Lane, London WC2A 1PL
Tel: 020 7242 1222
Website: www.lawsociety.org.uk

Lions Clubs
Order a single Message in a Bottle without charge
Tel: 0121 441 4544

Email: enquiries@lionsclubs.co
Website: www.lionsclubs.co/Public/messsage-in-a-bottle

Marie Curie
Provides frontline nursing and hospice care, a free support line and a wealth of information and support on all aspects of dying and death and bereavement
Tel: 0800 716 146
Email: supporter.relations@mariecurie.org.uk
Website: www.mariecurie.org.uk

MedicAlert
Medical ID jewellery containing your vital medical information, so first responders can make appropriate care decisions based on your individual needs
Tel: 01908 951045
Email: info@medicalert.org.uk
Website: www.medicalert.org.uk

Office of the Public Guardian
Provides information and guidance on making a power of attorney or applying to the Court of Protection
Tel: 0300 456 0300
Website: www.gov.uk/government/organisations/office-of-the-public-guardian

Organ Donation
The NHS Organ Donor Register is a secure database that keeps a record of your organ donation decision
NHS Blood and Transplant Organ Donation and Transplantation Directorate, Fox Den Road, Stoke

Gifford, Bristol BS34 8RR
Tel: 0300 123 23 23
Email: Enquiries@nhsbt.nhs.uk
Website: www.organdonation.nhs.uk/register-your-decision

Pushing Up The Daisies
A charity based in Scotland, enabling you to help you keep your loved one at home after their death
Tel: 0300 102 4444
Email: info@pushingupthedaisies.org.uk
Website: www.pushingupthedaisies.org.uk

The Silver Line
Confidential helpline providing information, friendship and advice to older people, open twenty-four hours a day, every day of the year.
Tel: 0800 4 70 80 90
Website: www.thesilverline.org.uk

Will Writing

Free Wills Month
Brings together a group of well-respected charities to offer members of the public aged fifty-five and over the opportunity to have simple wills written or updated free of charge
Website: www.freewillsmonth.org.uk

Institute of Professional Willwriters (IPW)
The recognised professional body regulating and promoting the profession of willwriting in England,

Wales and Northern Ireland
Institute of Professional Willwriters, Trinity Point, New Road, Halesowen, West Midlands B63 3HY
Tel: 0345 257 2570
Website: www.ipw.org.uk

National Will Register (Certainty)
Register your will so your beneficiaries can find it easily
Certainty The National Will Register, The Chapel, Chapel Lane, Lapworth, Solihull B94 6EU
Tel: 0330 100 3660
Email: enquiries@certainty.co.uk
Website: www.nationalwillregister.co.uk

The Society of Trust and Estate Practitioners (STEP)
The global professional association for those advising families across generations
Artillery House, 11–19 Artillery Row, London SW1P 1RT
Tel: 020 3752 3700
Email: step@step.org
Website: www.step.org

The Society of Will Writers (SWW)
The leading self-regulatory body for professional estate planners with over 1,700 members across the UK and also in Europe, Asia and Africa
The Society of Will Writers, Chancery House, Whisby Way, Lincoln LN6 3LQ
Tel: 01522 687888
Email: info@willwriters.com
Website: www.willwriters.com